Indexing Specialties:
HISTORY

EDITED BY MARGIE TOWERY

Indexing Specialties: HISTORY

EDITED BY MARGIE TOWERY

AMERICAN SOCIETY OF INDEXERS

ISBN 1-57387-055-2

Published by
Information Today, Inc.
143 Old Marlton Pike
Medford, NJ 08055

in association with

The American Society of Indexers, Inc.
PO Box 48267
Seattle, WA 98148-0267

Table of Contents

It's All in the Neighborhood: People, Place-Names,
  Concepts, and Terminology
  Introduction by Margie Towery ix

Saints, Kings, and Peasants: Indexing
  Medieval and Renaissance History
  Kate Mertes 1

Indexing Books on Latin American History
  Francine Cronshaw 11

Indexing History Textbooks
  Sandy Topping 17

Indexing Art and Art History Materials
  Marilyn Rowland and Diane Brenner 27

A Place in the Text: Gender and Sexual
  Orientation as Issues in Indexing History
  Victoria Baker 41

Helpful References on History: A General Bibliography 55

Contributors 59

Index 61

Preface

Indexing Specialties: History is the first in a series of publications from the American Society of Indexers focusing on the various areas in which indexers develop subject expertise and specialization. It is hoped that this series will provide continuing education for indexers and aid those who wish to learn the "finer" points of handling material in a given field. Each publication will consist of a group of articles written by experienced indexers who have practical advice to share as well as an overview of how to approach material in a particular subject area.

The American Society of Indexers would like to thank Margie Towery for the exemplary job she has done in compiling and editing the articles included in this publication. She also wrote the index. Our appreciation goes as well to the contributors: Kate Mertes, Francine Cronshaw, Sandy Topping, Marilyn Rowland and Diane Brenner, and Victoria Baker. The Contributors section tells a bit about each of them and is educational reading in and of itself.

We also want to acknowledge ITI and their staff for their able assistance in helping us publish this work. Both John Bryans and Rhonda Forbes are deserving of special mention.

Enid L. Zafran
Chair, Publication Committee
American Society of Indexers

IT'S ALL IN THE NEIGHBORHOOD:
PEOPLE, PLACE-NAMES, CONCEPTS, AND TERMINOLOGY

Margie Towery

Some folks might argue that indexing history materials is pretty straightforward. By indicating the depth—and variety—of knowledge needed in this specialty, the five articles included in this collection contradict that notion. Yet each article also provides recommendations on how and where to gain the needed information. These articles together are intended for a diverse audience: beginning indexers, indexers from other areas interested in expanding their work areas, and even, perhaps, editors and authors who must evaluate indexes.

Stylistic Concerns and Indexer Preferences

It's important to remember, however, that many components of an index are hotly debated among indexers (e.g., use of prepositions). Indeed, the contributors to this collection highlight just that, so readers will find some differences in examples among the articles. Many of these differences are purely stylistic—decisions made by the editor or publisher. But others are, I think, a matter of an indexer's particular style and preference. Over years of reading indexes and attending workshops, I have found that each indexer has her own style, just as writers do. (When I purchase a scholarly book, I am more likely to get the index read than the text!)

The examples included in the articles here are all presented in indented format, regardless of the published format, so that readers can more easily consider the author's point. Page locators vary from one article to another as well, with some elided and others not—a stylistic consideration usually made by the press. Another difference is in the location of the cross-references. For example, because I work primarily for scholarly presses, my indexes are almost always run-in, so I put my cross-references at the end, never at the top or after a subhead—that's a difference in both publisher guidelines and indexer preference.

I also think that each indexer develops a "stable" of favorite subheads. Mine include "role of," "description of," "structure of," and so on. This is an area where indexers show their personal preferences. I once had another indexer look at an index I had done and comment, "It looks like my indexes"—meaning that we had similar styles.

Another consideration is that every indexer must be true to the text with which he's working, a point Victoria Baker makes nicely. He must also develop a balance between producing a good index and what the clients request—whether marked by space limitations or demands for including entries that are unhelpful to readers. After all, if we don't keep our clients happy, we won't be able to continue to index—yet at heart (I hope), each indexer wants to turn out the best possible index under the contextual constraints of each project.

It's a Wonderful Day in the Neighborhood

At any rate, each of these articles will, we hope, foster discussion of both stylistic and personal preference considerations as well as address the issues of, as Sandy Topping puts it, the whos, whats, whens, wheres, and whys of history. When people asked me how I go about constructing or creating an index, I used to mention the analogy of a tree with its various branches (I've heard Fred Leise use this analogy). But I've since decided that a better analogy to what I do is that of a neighborhood.

A neighborhood has people who live there and people who visit. Visitors (index users) want to find people who live in the neighborhood (entries in the index). Sometimes those visitors are just delivering pizza—they want to get in and out really quick, maybe find out George Washington's birthplace, for example. Of course, they may consider it a tip if they also pick up some other information or become intrigued by another subject or "want to read more about" (so, OK, I'm an idealist when it comes to books). Or visitors may be there for a longer period, staying at someone's house, looking for a bit more information. Or they may be returnees: having left something behind, they want to make a quick, painless visit to pick it up—jog their memories. So the neighborhood must be accessible to each of the various kinds of visitors who might arrive.

We can extend this further, adding that some visitors will know the house number (term) they are looking for and others won't. For that reason, neighborhoods need streetlights (*See* references) to help people find their way, especially when they aren't aware of the text's terminology. They help visitors know where to go when they arrive at an empty weedy lot (of course, that empty lot could also be a concept in the text that's missing from the index).

Neighborhoods also need streets and sidewalks to connect the houses. These are the *See also* references that get visitors from one place to another, without leading them into one of those muddy potholes (read circular cross-references, etc.).

Many of the houses will have windows (subheads) so the visitor can peek in and see just where she wants to go. And of course, houses must have reliable house numbers—that is, alphabetical order.

Well, you get the picture of the neighborhood analogy. That said, I might add that my own "real" neighborhood has neither sidewalks nor streetlights. But my indexes do! And the samples of indexes in these pages do, as well.

Indexing History Materials

Each contributor deals with many of these questions—people, places, concepts, and terminology—in terms of a specific content area within history. The five articles may seem like an odd collection—they were selected by virtue of their authors' willingness to give freely of their time and energy. The articles are not intended to be the last word either on indexing history or even on indexing in that content area. They are intelligent, sensitive discussions of issues that indexers face in a variety of history materials.

Moreover, each article reaches across specialty areas with implications for all indexing, both of history texts and of texts in other fields. No doubt those who index works on music history will find Diane Brenner and Marilyn Rowland's article on art and art history materials of considerable interest, since it deals with artists and their works. Kate Mertes's article on medieval and Renaissance history is an excellent starting point in that area and highlights many useful strategies for getting up to speed in new areas (e.g., reading other indexes and books in the area). Sandy Topping's lucid description of indexing history textbooks reaches across into other subjects as well—and gives us a glimpse into her actual indexing process. Francine Cronshaw's consideration of Latin American history materials reminds us of the careful attention we must pay to culture and names in any area. Victoria Baker's article serves as an overarching viewpoint, illustrating the critical importance of attention to language in every index.

Each contributor was willing to consider and write about her concerns in her topic. I offer my heartfelt thanks to each of them for their wonderful, timely contributions.

SAINTS, KINGS, AND PEASANTS:
INDEXING MEDIEVAL AND RENAISSANCE HISTORY

Kate Mertes

College-level students facing their first course in medieval and Renaissance history are often frustrated by the subject matter. While they may have worked with sixteenth-century materials, most high-school students have never really dealt with much medieval and early Renaissance history, and it is often a big surprise. Suddenly they are confronted with languages they don't readily understand, documents that are usually impersonal and opaque to the general reader, historical concepts and terms with which they are unfamiliar, and—most disconcertingly—a very alien worldview. As one of my students once said to me, having wrestled with an essay on attitudes about death in fourteenth-century England, "I just don't *get* these people."

Indexers facing their first medieval or Renaissance history text may feel the same way. This essay is designed to help ease an indexer into the field with some idea of what to expect and how to handle this often difficult but always challenging historical period. Both novice indexers who've never done a history text and experienced indexers of history and social studies who have not dealt with these earlier periods should find useful information about how to approach a medieval or Renaissance text.

Does Anybody Really Know What Time It Is?

Just what are the medieval and Renaissance periods? What time period can you expect to be working on? Unfortunately, there is no straight answer to this. The widest view is probably around 300 to around 1600 A.D., but most historians construe the time in question in a more restricted fashion. The beginning of the medieval period may be given as around 300, relating it to the reign of the Roman Emperor Constantine the Great, whose vision at the battle of the Milvian Bridge in 312 is popularly viewed as the beginning of established Christianity and whose founding of Constantinople, or New Rome, in 330 effectively split the old empire in two (Collins 1991). The years 409, the date of the withdrawal of Roman troops from Britain, or about 476, the end of the reign of the last emperor in Rome, are also common choices signifying the end of the antique era and the beginning of the Middle Ages. But many historians really don't consider this early period to be medieval. Known as the Dark Ages, due to lack of political and social stability and also to the very small number of surviving documents, this spread of time often is not covered by texts on the medieval period. Older or more conservative historians may refer to the period after the fall of Rome as the Late Antique, but the same term is also used by scholars of ancient history to refer to the latter years of the Roman Empire, from Julius Caesar or Augustus Caesar (the first emperors) to about 476.

English medieval history is often considered to commence about 1066, when William the Conqueror became king of England. European historians are more likely to go with the pope's crowning of Charlemagne as emperor (800). One older but still-respected theory argues that Charlemagne's reign indicates a fundamental shift of European interests away from the Mediterranean basin as the center of trade and culture (Pirenne 1958, 282-85), and hence a decisive break with the Roman world.

If what constitutes the beginning of the medieval period is a vexed question, when it ends is even more confusing. What is sometimes called the High Middle Ages, the flowering of culture and art and the stabilization of society and economy in the thirteenth century, is considered the Renaissance (or a renaissance) by some historians. For many art historians and students of Italian history, the fourteenth century is the beginning of the Renaissance. For scholars of English history, the sixteenth century is the Renaissance, covering the Tudor dynasty in England, from the defeat of Richard III by Henry VII in 1475 to the end of Elizabeth I's reign (1603). Ecclesiastical historians may consider the splintering of Europe's religious cohesion, often known as the Reformation, to be more or less synonymous with the Renaissance period. Linguists sometimes look at the shift away from Latin and toward the vernacular, around the beginning of the fifteenth century, as the start of the Renaissance. The term "early modern" is beginning to overtake "renaissance" in application to historical works about Northern Europe in the fifteenth and sixteenth centuries. However, for historians of the seventeenth and eighteenth centuries, early modern can denote anything from the late sixteenth century through the beginning of the industrial revolution in the early eighteenth century; and for scholars of ancient history, early modern means the fourth through the eighteenth centuries.

No decent historian really regards any of these dates as hard-and-fast rules. As with our modern penchant for characterizing each decade of the twentieth century, labels such as "medieval," "early modern," "renaissance," and "dark ages" are signifiers of modal changes occurring gradually over time. A writer working in English literary history who considers the Middle Ages to be the twelfth through the fifteenth centuries may very well spend time talking about both Beowulf (ninth or tenth century) and Shakespeare (sixteenth and seventeenth centuries). The indexer, however, needs to understand the different conceptualizations of "medieval" and "renaissance" in order to anticipate just what the book to be indexed is going to cover.

All Roads *Don't* Lead to Rome

The alert reader will have noticed that all the events referred to in determining the time span of the medieval and Renaissance periods occur in Europe. The entire concept of the Middle Ages and Renaissance is a Eurocentric one, derived as a way of understanding those countries that were once part of the Roman Empire. In terms of geography and influence, the further one gets from the boundaries of the old *imperium*, the less and less applicable is the continuum implied by medieval/renaissance—the dying empire, chaos, rebuilding, rebirth.

The ideas of "medieval" and "renaissance" are ways of framing time for a cultural unit. They are problematic for areas we now tend to class as European but that were beyond the fringe of Roman influence—the states that would become Russia and the Scandinavian countries, for instance. Islamic historians concentrating on the Middle East and North Africa sometimes use the notions of a medieval and Renaissance period; these areas were, after all, subject to the influence of Rome and underwent some of the chaos and rejuvenation consequent to its fall. But these time frames really are quite inapplicable for Africa, the Americas, and most of Asia. Historians do sometimes talk of, say, "medieval Africa," but only in the context of its relationship to Europe. African historians divide and order time quite differently. So an indexer can be fairly sure that any book with "medieval," "Middle Ages," or "Renaissance" in the title will be about Europe.

To Market, To Market

There are not many children's books about the Middle Ages. Most beginners' texts for the medieval and Renaissance period are aimed at college students who are already familiar with considerable historical theory. Thus, a method of entry useful to indexers in other fields—the beginners' or child's text—is effectively denied. General textbooks covering the period do exist (especially for art history), and often medieval and Renaissance period material is incorporated into textbooks covering a wider time period (general histories of a particular country, for example, or a specific subject, such as marriage and family). However, the vast majority of books published on the Middle Ages and Renaissance are either monographs or thematically based essay collections aimed at advanced college students and specialists in the field rather than beginners or the general public. Biographies of individuals and of lineages (a history of the Dukes of Buckingham, for instance) are also not uncommon.

Certainly this makes determining readership a fairly easy task for the indexer. The market for these books is largely academic, so developing cross-references from more general terms for the average reader won't be much of a problem. However, it does provide difficulties for the indexer new to the period. The indexer who wants to work on medieval or Renaissance texts can best break into the field by stressing disciplinary strengths. For instance, an indexer who has worked on nineteenth-century women's history can advertise experience in that field to editors of medieval and Renaissance texts. Much of the theoretical terminology of women's history generally will carry over into works on the earlier period. The time period may be foreign, but the subject matter will provide some handles on the text.

Indexers who have never worked on a historical text are probably best advised not to start with the Middle Ages unless they have an academic background or have read extensively in the field. Renaissance and early modern history are closer to our thought patterns and worldview and hence often more accessible to the indexer (and the reader) new to history and historical theory. An exception to this may be art history. General textbooks on medieval and Renaissance art are not uncommon, and an indexer with any experience with books on art will probably find this avenue a useful (as well as aesthetically and intellectually stimulating) way to ease gradually into earlier historical periods.

Taking the Plunge

Let's say you've gotten your first early historical text to index. It's a book of essays on contagious diseases in the Middle Ages, covering epidemics from eighth-century

Constantinople to early sixteenth-century England. There are twelve different authors. The publisher is planning to market it for college courses as well as the professorial audience. You've indexed a popular book on emerging diseases and have some background in medical textbooks and nineteenth-century history. How do you prepare for this new project?

First, you need to ask the editor some questions. How many pages do you have to work with? Academic monographs and essay collections usually run 200-350 pages and allow 8-16 pages for the index. Different presses prefer different styles; most seem to prefer run-in these days, but some presses require indented indexes. This will allow you to gauge the depth of indexing you can attempt from a purely practical point of view. You also need to ask the editor about the "slant" of the book. Feminism, Marxism (an old school, but still influential), or any other philosophical approach to history tends to have its own terminology and themes that the indexer needs to be familiar with and to cover in the index.

Next, it would be a good idea to get to a library. If you live near a university, you might be able to get reading privileges for a small fee; this will grant you access to a wide range of the most recent books. The library is a great place to check out related texts and their indexes. Emergent disease, for instance, has recently spawned a whole genre of books across a number of disciplines, and aimed at everyone from a popular readership to academics (Garrett 1994). Checking out these books will give you a sense of the concerns and concepts that current books on diseases are likely to cover and hence what your readers might want to look up.

While you're at the library, you should look at a wide range of books concerned with the medieval period, whether or not they are in your subject area. Try to look at recent books, no more than seven years old. You'll be able to spot common themes that run across different topics. The family, for instance, continues to be a popular topic in medieval history (Goody 1983), and your project may contain minor strains on this theme (the stress epidemics place on family structure, for instance) that you might ignore if you weren't aware of it as something readers might look for. Don't forget academic journals (such as *English Historical Review, Bulletin of the Institute of Historical Research, American Historical Review,* and *Speculum*); they'll give you the most current picture of what people are writing about just now.

Now you've prepared by gaining some familiarity with the time period, the subject matter, and philosophical school covered by your project. The FedEx truck has just dropped off your page proofs. What else do you need to be aware of? Every indexer working with medieval/Renaissance texts needs to be ready for four especially knotty areas: language, spelling, names, and terminology.

You Say Middle Ages, I Say *Medium Aevum*

One of the biggest challenges for students of the Middle Ages is the linguistic hurdle. While vernacular languages of the modern period have their own historical peculiarities, generally, if one is working in English history, one only need know English. However, medievalists must be able to work with texts in Old English (practically unrecognizable to the modern English speaker) and/or Middle English (closer to modern

English, but not that close), depending on the time period; Latin, of course (medieval Latin, not classical—the tenses are much simplified, the vocabulary and spelling is different, and the cases are a mess, largely rendered redundant by the use of prepositions); the Anglo-French spoken by English people post-Norman conquest (similar to but not quite the same as Middle French as spoken in Normandy); and the Anglo-French used as the official language of English law (a rule entirely unto itself). Depending upon one's area of study, one might need to conquer Welsh or the distinctive dialects of Northern England.

Students of France, Germany, Italy, and all other European countries face the same sorts of linguistic problems. Fortunately for the indexer, most publishers now require the inclusion of modern English translations of all dialects and languages quoted in historical texts; the indexer of medieval history need not be a polyglot (although it helps). However, the indexer does need to make choices about which words to index. For instance, in the same text, Christine de Pizan's best-known work, *Livre de la Cité des Dames,* may be referred to as this its French title and also by its common English translation, *Book of the City of Ladies* ([1405] 1982). A book on English law may refer to both the Parliament Rolls and the *Rotuli Parliamentorum* (1767-77). The indexer will have to make decisions, based on frequency of use and perhaps the book's market, as to which term will be preferred and which will be cross-referenced in the index.

Some knowledge of Latin is extremely useful to the indexer of medieval texts. Indexers working in the Renaissance period, which is characterized by the rise of the vernacular languages, will have less need of linguistic skills but will still find themselves sometimes mired in difficulties created by a plethora of languages.

How Do I Love Thee? Let Me Spell the Ways . . .

If language can be a problem, spelling can be a major obstacle for indexers, who rely on standardized conventions to order their work. Until well into the seventeenth century, people basically just spelled words as they spoke them. Both medieval and Renaissance texts reflect the speech patterns and dialectic idiosyncrasies of the writer or scribe. Indeed, writers of this period are seldom even internally consistent in their spelling habits, often writing the same word two or more different ways in the same paragraph. Sir Walter Raleigh, for instance, is famous for spelling his own name at least twenty-three different ways (in fact, modern writers still quarrel over whether to spell it as Raleigh or Ralegh—you'll find both used). During the very early medieval period scribes didn't even leave spaces between words: imagine-try-ing-to-read-let-a-lone-in-dex-lines-like-this (Romer 1988, illustrations at 264 [plates 30 and 32], 271, 229).

While historians will translate quotes in nonmodern languages, they generally do not give modern versions of idiosyncratically spelled but understandable passages used in their texts. The indexer needs to read such passages carefully; it can be very easy to miss an occurrence of an important concept when veiled in unfamiliar spelling. Adding to the difficulty, historians are fond of pulling out an archaic or oddly spelled word from a pivotal text and using it alongside a modern equivalent. Recently, in a medieval feminist history I indexed, one author repeatedly used the word "quiting" (which can be roughly translated as "getting back at"), pulled from a Chaucerian reference to Eve, as well as "revenge" and a number of other related modern terms (Weisl 1998). I needed to make choices about what the reader was likely to look up—both the first-time reader looking for the overall concept and the repeat reader coming back to the book and looking for that specific term—in order to construct a flexible indexing structure that would accommodate all comers. I put the entries under "quiting" and cross-referenced from Eve, revenge, and several other terms used in the text.

What's in a Name?

Earlier I mentioned Christine de Pizan. How would one index her? If she were a modern person, the indexer would be trying to decide between "de" and "Pizan." However, neither "de Pizan" nor "Pizan" is Christine's last name. She's a medieval person who does not really have a surname. "De Pizan" indicates details of her place of origin and birthright and is specific to her. Her son's name was Jean de Castel. Similarly, Thomas Aquinas was not Tom, son of Harry and Lucy Aquinas—his name was Thomas, and he was from Aquino. Margaret of Anjou is a member of the noble house of Anjou. So Christine is indexed as "Christine de Pizan," not "Pizan, Christine de"; Thomas is indexed as "Thomas Aquinas" and not "Aquinas, Thomas"; Margaret is listed as "Margaret of Anjou," not "Anjou, Margaret."

However, just to confuse the issue, some medieval persons *did* have last names. Surnames begin to crop up in the eleventh to the thirteenth centuries; John Teal, a former teacher of mine and a Byzantine scholar, was fond of quoting the example of a Robert the Gross and his son John the Gross. Robert was very fat. His son John used the appellation "the Gross," despite the fact that he was very thin, as a way of indicating his descent. This is the beginning of a surname. If your last name is Reeve, chances are if you could go back far enough you'd find an actual reeve (a manorial official) and a descendant who was not a reeve but who used Reeve as part of his or her name anyway. If, however, your last name is Duke, don't get any illusions of grandeur. Such surnames are more likely to derive from nicknames than from royal descent. If John Wayne had been an actor in the Middle Ages, his children might have taken the surname Duke rather than Wayne.

Actual surnames increase in frequency as one nears the modern period. If a person has an actual surname, then they are listed under the last name rather than the first name ("Bordet, Robert," not "Robert Bordet"). Usually one can tell by how an appendage is used as to whether it is a real surname, but it is not always obvious, especially if one is dealing with the High Middle Ages (1200-1500). Are there relatives with the same surname? Does the person come from the place indicated as the appended title? If in doubt, the best thing to do is to check the indexes to several other books on the same period or subject. If this does not clarify matters, call the editor or author.

While some sticklers don't agree with this, I always put in a double-posting or a cross-reference from the appendage. The experienced reader will know that Christine de Pizan is under Christine, but one must allow for those readers who think of Pizan first. I also consider whether I need a cross-reference or double-posting for an alternative version of a name. Some persons are known by a different name in other countries, and while they may turn out to be very close to each other in the index (Thomas Aquinas/Thomaso d'Aquino, for instance), if the book being indexed uses both terms, the index must accommodate that. This is especially true for literary characters such as those in the Arthurian legends, who may have many name variants.

Titled persons are treated rather differently. Generally, Henry, Duke of Buckingham would be listed under Buckingham, not under his first name (or under "Duke"). However, nobles with a family name must be cross-referenced. If the Duke of Buckingham in question was Henry Stafford, for instance, the index requires a cross-reference from "Stafford, Henry, Duke of Buckingham," to "Buckingham, Dukes of." If the text was actually about the Dukedom of Buckingham, however, one might want to index the different lineages under their patronymics rather than under the title:

> Buckingham, Dukes of
> Stafford family. *See* Stafford Dukes of Buckingham

And if one were dealing only with the Stafford Dukes of Buckingham, one might very well decide to index them by first name—with appropriate indicators of individuality, since many of them have the same name (*Chicago Manual* 1993, 734 [17.82-83]).

Kings are not listed under their title (not England, Henry I, King of) or rank (King Henry I) but under their first names (Henry I). If one is dealing with a book covering both England and France, however, one may want to list kings called Henry as Henry I and Henri I, or Henry I of England and Henry I of France, depending on whether or not the author uses the Francophone spelling (ibid., 734 [17.81-82]).

Ecclesiastical titles are treated similarly. Bishops and archbishops are indexed as for nobles: "Nola, Paulinus, Bishop of"; "MacGregor, James, Archbishop of Glasgow. *See* Glasgow, Archbishop of." Popes are listed in the same way as kings (John Paul II) (ibid., 734, 735 [17.81, 17.85]). The indexer may need to insert clarifying phrases if a plethora of names results in kings and popes with the same name: "Leo X of Hesse," "Leo X (Pope)."

Saints generally are listed under their names rather than by title: "Augustine of Hippo," "Borromeo, Charles." You may or may not want to indicate their spiritual status, as in: "Thomas Aquinas (saint)," depending on the text and readership (ibid., 735 [17.88]). However, in a book that contains sections on the notion of sainthood but does not contain many saints' names, you might also want to double-post or cross-reference individuals under saints—for example, you might want entries for Lucy (Virgin Martyr) and Philomela (Virgin Martyr), and St. Lucy and St. Philomela.

I can imagine odd circumstances in which one might be similarly tempted to create lists of other people by title: kings, bishops, popes, or dukes. In most cases, however, such lists are not terribly useful to the reader, unless the book deals with the concept of kingship or popedom and does not mention very many persons carrying such titles or talk about them at length. Usually historians are interested in locating individuals through the index, not all bishops or all dukes mentioned in the text.

All these circumstances apply even more so, of course, to the indexer working on a biography of a person in the Middle Ages or Renaissance. Generally such works follow the same rules applicable to any biographical index, although biographies of nobles present an extreme version of the problem that indexers face with any person whose name changes over time. A biography of Henry IV of England, for instance, will likely cover the period of his life when he was Henry, Earl of Derby. The indexer is best advised to consult with the author as to how to handle this switch. Some indexes may have entries under "Derby, Earl of" and "Henry IV," with cross-references; others may put all biographical entries under "Henry IV" and have a separate entry for "Derby, Earldom of" that deals only with material on the earldom's lands, its conveyance, and so on. The structure and aim of the book may determine which works best (ibid., 734 [17.83]).

A Rose by Any Other Name . . .

Many indexers have real trouble dealing with the terminology of medieval and Renaissance history, especially when the work to be indexed is a collection of essays by multiple authors. While some historical writing is refreshingly free of jargon, in general, historians of the medieval and Renaissance periods are fond of coining phrases. Thematically oriented writing (a book on twelfth-century concepts of sexuality, for instance, as opposed to a work on the reign of Robert the Bruce), historical interpretations based on literature, and texts closely allied with a philosophical school (feminism, Marxism) are most likely to produce terminological conundrums; narrative history is more likely to be jargon-free and easier to deal with for the indexer new to medieval and Renaissance history.

Much of this terminological tangle is a necessary evil. These writers are dealing with novel and complex theory; like computer-speak, reducing it to "plain English" is just impossible. However, some authors are rather fond of ideologisms—they coin terms that no one else uses and that they themselves use only in the context of a single twenty-page article. How do you as an indexer handle this? First, examine similar texts and their indexes. If you're dealing with a work based on feminist theory, take a look at other women's history books. You'll soon have an idea of what terms are common to this school of thought, which are variations, and which are completely unique. You'll still have to index all of them, but you'll know better what should be used as the main entry and what should be cross-referenced. "Normalization of violence," for instance, was a key concept in a text I recently indexed; it's also an accepted element of feminist theory. In the book of essays I was indexing, however, several of the authors used "naturalization" rather than "normalization." I put the entries under the latter and cross-referenced from the former (Roberts 1998).

Be aware that terminology, like fashion, has its fads. When I was a graduate student, the head of the history department threatened to flay alive anyone who used the word "paradigm" again. At the moment, "hermeneutics" and "teleology" seem to be favorites. These are perfectly decent words in themselves, and they may last as concepts that a historian might want to look up, or they may fade from the historical vocabulary. The astute indexer will recognize such terms and try to include cross-referencing synonyms for these concepts when they require indexing, in order to keep the book usable over a longer period of time.

Conclusion

You've just finished indexing that work on contagious disease in the Middle Ages. You may be ready to throw the book across the room in frustration, or you may be totally enthralled and desperate to do more. If you reveled in this strange world and want to index more medieval and Renaissance history, continuing education is an extremely good idea. Ask a university history department for the reading list for their beginning class on early European history—and start reading.

Go to conferences and meetings, local and national—this is a good way to both bone up on the latest thinking in the field and to meet prospective clients. Every year in Kalamazoo there is a huge international conference on the Middle Ages and Renaissance, stretching over five days, with over three hundred papers given. Local historical societies and almost every college or university that teaches medieval or Renaissance history will have occasional evening lecture series and day or weekend seminars that indexers can attend. Start looking at primary sources: the literature, chronicles, and daily records that form the basis for historical thought (Rosenthal 1976).

Medieval history is definitely an acquired taste. While many people enjoy reading about the Renaissance, the Middle Ages is truly another country that can be very hard to understand or relate to. Few people in the Middle Ages indulged (in writing) in the sort of emotional expression and introspection we allow ourselves; not many letters and journals survive, and those that do are often highly impersonal, dealing more with immediate needs and day-to-day functions than with thoughts or feelings. As a result we can only view medieval people through the veil of their actions, and interpreting these can be difficult. As another of my students once told me after finishing an essay on the Flagellants, a religious movement in which participants ritually beat themselves in public, "These people are *weird.*" Medieval people are rather strange from our point of view; they looked at the world very differently from the way we do. This is the biggest hurdle of all for the indexer as it is for the historian, but also the most fascinating aspect of indexing medieval and Renaissance texts.

Works Cited

Chicago Manual of Style. 1993. 14th ed. Chicago: University of Chicago Press.

Christine de Pizan. [1405] 1982. *The Book of the City of Ladies.* Trans. Earl Jeffrey Richards. New York: Persea.

Collins, Roger. 1991. *Early Medieval Europe, 300-1000.* New York: St. Martin's Press.

Garrett, Laurie. 1994. *The Coming Plague.* New York: Farrar, Straus, and Giroux.

Goody, Jack. 1983. *The Development of the Family and Marriage in Europe.* Cambridge: Cambridge University Press.

Pirenne, Henri. 1958. *Mohammed and Charlemagne.* London: George Allen and Unwin.

Roberts, Anna, ed. 1998. *Violence against Women in Medieval Texts.* Gainesville: University Press of Florida.

Romer, John. 1988. *Testament: The Bible and History.* New York: Henry Holt.

Rotuli Parliamentorum. 1767-77. 6 vols. London: HMSO [a CD-ROM version is in preparation but the original transcription, available in most college libraries, is remarkably accurate].

Rosenthal, Joel. 1976. *Nobles and the Noble Life, 1295-1500.* London: George Allen and Unwin [provides an interesting introduction to primary sources with a wide array of documents].

Weisl, Angela Jane. 1998. "Quiting Eve: Violence against Women in the *Canterbury Tales.*" Pp. 115-36 in *Violence against Women,* ed. Roberts.

INDEXING BOOKS ON LATIN AMERICAN HISTORY

Francine Cronshaw

The majority of books written about Latin America and published in the United States are written by academic types, whether teachers at colleges and universities or independent scholars. A smaller number of Latin American titles are released by trade or independent presses. Whether scholarly or general interest press, the publisher is likely to provide some guidelines (more rarely, a style sheet for your particular project) for formatting your index. A good part of the following discussion will, I hope, help indexers make better use of publisher guidelines by illuminating some of the issues unique to the field. Before embarking on the finer points, however, it may be useful to look at the historical context of Latin American studies, with an emphasis on second-language (Spanish and Portuguese) issues.

For those new to Latin American studies, the term, as it is used in academic circles, refers to research conducted in the fields of history, sociology, economics, urban planning, political science, literary criticism, anthropology, and so forth. Spanish (and Portuguese) language and literature can also be included under the rubric of Latin American studies but will not be considered in this essay.

Latin America is one of several major regions of the world considered worthy of "area study." Other regions routinely studied under the area study convention are the Middle East, Africa, Asia, and Eastern Europe. Academic interest in the so-called Third World increased dramatically after World War II. According to cold war thinking, information about other regions of the world was vital to the U.S. "national interest." The world was viewed as divided into two major ideological blocs—either of which would prove irresistible as a role model to the rest of the countries of the world, according to the cold war worldview. Thus, knowledge about other cultures, especially those of the Third World, was a necessary preemptive measure to head off the perceived threat of Soviet influence. The other reason was economic: the twentieth century was the "American century," and economic intelligence was vital to the penetration of smaller nations by multinational corporations. (And yes, even a decade after the fall of the Berlin Wall, economic intelligence gathering remains a major justification for the CIA's continued existence.)

The academic field of Latin American studies had a major boost during John F. Kennedy's administration, when the perceived threat of the Cuban Revolution (and its purported demonstration effect on the rest of Latin America) prompted the creation of the Alliance for Progress. Whatever the merits of the Alliance as a typical trickle-down foreign aid program, its domestic effects, especially in education, were substantial. The Alliance for Progress created Title VI, a program to fund area studies in U.S. universities. A number of Latin American centers were created, and scholars received funding to conduct a wide variety of field research, such as assessing the revolutionary potential of Bolivian peasants.

11

The overall effect of Title VI was to attract a greater number of better-qualified students and scholars to the study of other nations. It also had the effect of improving foreign language skills in the scholarly community. In history, for example, previous generations of historians writing about Latin America usually had reading skills only in Spanish or Portuguese, library-centered skills used in researching their books on military, diplomatic, and political themes. The 1960s generation and subsequent generations of Latin Americanists, however, expected to speak and even write Spanish or Portuguese, in addition to their language research skills. Often some degree of *compromiso* (political commitment) to the region influenced their attitudes toward language and culture acquisition. A pronounced New Left orientation, reflected in historical materialist assumptions, continues to inform scholarship on Latin America.

Higher standards for foreign-language use in academic circles have had a commensurate effect in scholarly publishing, as those trained in recent generations move into leadership positions within their respective presses. It is still very common, however, to find that many presses do not have a single bilingual copyeditor or native Spanish speaker on staff. A skilled freelance indexer can thus offer much-needed abilities and assist with quality control in the production of books on Latin American topics.

The increasing level of mastery of Spanish (and Portuguese) among authors and academics has had a direct impact on manuscripts in English. Though written in the English language, books are likely to follow Spanish-language conventions in three major ways: (1) use of appropriate accent marks, (2) use of Spanish terms and concepts that are not easily translatable, and (3) use of Spanish citation style in bibliographic entries in that language. All three of the above may raise consistency questions for the indexer, because they are presented in more than one fashion in the text.

Accent marks inconsistently used by the author and not attended to by the line editor turn into a thorny area for an indexer whose grasp of Spanish is not strong. If the publisher provides a style sheet, the indexer has at least a good start on many of the inconsistent spellings that may be present. A good Spanish dictionary will help (*Simon and Schuster's International Dictionary English/Spanish–Spanish/English,* for example, is excellent). Remember, however, that the Spanish language has approximately five times as many words as English. Thus, any dictionary consulted may or may not contain the arcane or recent usages you seek to verify. In addition, many regional usages exist throughout Latin America and even within the same country. For example, the recently released *Diccionario del español usual en México* (1996) does not show regional usages from states such as Zacatecas or Chiapas. Place-names can be checked for spelling accuracy in *Webster's New Geographical Dictionary.* Given that the text's language is English, it would be more appropriate to use "Peru," rather than "Perú" to refer to the Andean nation. One also finds the country of El Salvador listed under the article (El) in the "E" section. (Article use tends to be especially thorny, and reference works can provide ready—if not always consistent—answers.)

When all else fails and the indexer is not sure if a particular name or term carries an accent mark or not, partly because the author has used them inconsistently, she can always cite them in the index as they appear in the text, for example, "Bolivar, Simon, 36"; "Bolívar, Simón, 87, 245." With a note from the indexer that spelling inconsistencies have been flagged in the index, the editor can then easily find inconsistent usages where they occurred in both text and index.

Many concepts and terms that describe another culture cannot be translated adequately into English. The current protocol is that the first time such concepts or terms are introduced, they appear in italics. Subsequent mentions of the same concept or term generally appear in roman. In the index, italicized terms or concepts usually follow the author's initial usage (italicized), although the indexer should be aware of many foreign words that have crept into daily English and do not require italicization (e.g., coup de grace, caudillo). Novices might note that individual publishers generally have their own rules in this regard. As is the case generally, to check whether a term you suspect might be considered to be in common usage, look it up in *Webster's Collegiate Dictionary* (most recent edition). Any accent marks that appear in the term or concept in the text should be replicated exactly in the index entry.

Occasionally the indexer will encounter citations of books or articles in the body of the work. Depending on the approach adopted, many times those citations do not find their way into the index. If they do, the indexer should be aware that the correct form for a book title in Spanish is capitalizing the first word (whether noun, article, or verb) and leaving all other words, except proper nouns, in lower case. Examples are *Cien años de soledad* (Gabriel García Márquez) or *Colonización y conflicto: Las lecciones de Sumapaz* (Elsy Marulanda).

Naming in Spanish

Citing names in the index in Spanish and Portuguese offers special challenges. Because the two languages have radically different approaches and the majority of books published in the U.S. context contain Spanish rather than Portuguese references, emphasis here will be on Spanish naming protocols. Despite the similarities between the two languages and the large number of cognates (words that look alike) that they share, their naming systems bear no relationship to one another.

Only recently have newspapers and other sectors of the mass media started to cite Spanish surnames correctly. Previously, confusion between the father's last name (patronymic) and the mother's last name (matronymic) was rife. In Spanish, a person often has a compound (or double) first name, such as José Luis or Luz Marina, but he may choose to use only one given name (Constanza). Usually, however, people use two last names: the father's surname or family name, followed by the mother's family name. Thus, the Nobel laureate in literature is Gabriel García Márquez. His father's family name, García, is as common as Smith in U.S. culture. Márquez is his mother's family name. García Márquez (or Gabo, as he is known in Colombia) probably has two given names but chooses to use only Gabriel. The index citation would read:

García Márquez, Gabriel, 81, 103, 116–43

While the above is the general protocol for naming in Spanish and covers most of the cases the indexer is likely to encounter, a few exceptions need to be noted. Leading historical figures are often known by a single surname, such as Diego Rivera (the artist) or Emiliano Zapata and José Martí (the revolutionaries). A single surname is also preferred by persons who would affect a more modern usage and by others whose mother's family name has less luster in a class-conscious context.

The authoritative name reference for Latin American studies is the *HAPI Thesaurus and Name Authority, 1970–1989* (Valk 1989) from UCLA's Latin American Center. The *Name Authority* is 300 pages of personal names that include the name of anyone who has written about Latin America in recent decades in addition to leading historical figures. Thus, we find the sixteenth-century priest who denounced Spanish abuse of the indigenous population of Santo Domingo listed as "Casas, Bartolomé de las." The former dictator of Cuba appears as "Batista y Zaldivar, Fulgencio" (often one sees "Batista, Fulgencio"). Many Latin American authors are included in the list.

Brazilian Portuguese names are relatively simple. The final surname guides the alphabetization (such as Sérgio da Costa Franco, which becomes "Franco, Sérgio da Costa"). Exceptions, using a double surname, reflect well-known figures from the nineteenth century or earlier eras. The author's usage in the body of the text should help the indexer in most cases.

Access to a name authority or similarly authoritative source can prove a challenge. Research libraries at universities, especially those dozen or so universities with Latin American centers, are sure to keep a print copy in their reference section (meaning you can't check it out and will have to use it on site). The most recent edition of HAPI's *Thesaurus and Name Authority* came out in 1989. Currently, it is moving to an electronic format. According to Barbara Valk, the number of names in the name authority has increased by at least 50 percent since 1989, and a subsequent edition has been held up by printing costs. The 1989 version is still available for approximately $45.00 (call UCLA's distribution center at 310/825-6634 or contact Ms. Valk at her e-mail address: bvalk@ucla.edu).

Another source is the five-volume *Encyclopedia of Latin American History and Culture* (1996). Its index, located in the final volume, is over a hundred pages long and has many of the historical figures and events that an indexer of Latin American history topics might seek to verify. It also seems to be more intuitive in the sense that it is guided by reader usages rather than by library cataloging rules (such as Las Casas, Bartolomé de). Other resources perhaps more readily available but less complete in terms of the present discussion are *The Cambridge Encyclopedia of Latin America and the Caribbean* (2d ed., 1992) and Ernest E. Rossi and Jack C. Plano, *Latin America: A Political Dictionary* (1992). The Cambridge encyclopedia covers a range of social science and art history as well as history topics, and the index (like the book itself) is relatively brief.

Indexing Content

Like any other type of indexing, one's skill in indexing Latin American history ultimately depends on knowledge of the academic field as well as an adequate command of Spanish and/or Portuguese. There really are no shortcuts to the type of quality control that an indexer with a good background in the subject area can provide (for those readers who think they might be sensing an implicit argument in favor of specialization, they are).

Indexing textbooks does not require a specialized knowledge of the area because of the structure of textbooks and how they are used to communicate information. Academic monographs, on the other hand, often contain more tortured phrasing and convoluted arguments. The indexer's knowledge of which names and events are significant and which epochs and approaches are implicit rather than specified in the text (and making the implicit explicit with cross-references) helps create a stronger index.

Whatever the extent of their backgrounds, indexers wishing to keep their clients content will pay close attention to editorial guidelines. While guidelines most often indicate the preferred format for indexes, they may also stipulate general approaches for selecting content. For example, editors at one scholarly press feel that an index should not be a substitute for reading the book. Thus, if a chapter deals with a specific topic, such as machismo, it would not be appropriate to break it down into its subtopics. The subtopics and major related concepts, however, may be suitably cited. Emphasis is merited here: Indexers who want to keep their clients contented with indexes they produce will pay close attention to client guidelines and try to understand the thinking behind them. As experienced indexers well know, publisher guidelines can be a trial and occasionally seem to interfere with the indexer's sense of what is appropriate and correct. Thus at times the fit between a competent representation of a book's content and the limitations imposed by the publisher on a particular project is somewhat uneasy. Finding that fit sometimes makes indexing feel more like an art than a science.

Works Cited

Bethell, Leslie, ed. 1984-95. *Cambridge History of Latin America.* 11 vols. New York: Cambridge University Press [though the indexes in each volume contain occasional flaws, the series of eleven paperbacks is an excellent in-depth reference work].

The Cambridge Encyclopedia of Latin America and the Caribbean. 1992. 2d ed. New York: Cambridge University Press.

Diccionario del español usual en México. 1996. Mexico, DF: Colegio de México.

Rossi, Ernest E., and Jack C. Plano, eds. 1992. *Latin America: A Political Dictionary.* Santa Barbara, Calif.: ABC-CLIO.

Simon and Schuster's International Dictionary English/Spanish–Spanish/English. 1997. Roger J. Steiner, editor in chief. New York: Macmillan.

Tenenbaum, Barbara A., ed. 1996. *Encyclopedia of Latin American History and Culture.* New York: Charles Scribner's Sons.

Valk, Barbara, ed. 1989. *HAPI Thesaurus and Name Authority, 1970-1989.* Los Angeles: University of California, Latin American Center.

Webster's New Geographical Dictionary. 1988. Springfield, Mass.: Merriam-Webster.

INDEXING HISTORY TEXTBOOKS

Sandy Topping

Note: I have included a step-by-step outline of my textbook indexing process (appendix B). I have tried to be as detailed as possible, including everything a beginning indexer might need to do. It may appear to be time-consuming but many of the steps take very little time in practice. My average time for a history text—start to finish—is 8-10 pages per hour.

"Constance Reader"

When indexing history texts, the most important person is the reader. Whether it's a freshman-level text or an advanced, graduate-level volume, the indexer must assume that the material will be entirely new to the student. I try to imagine that my quintessential student is writing a term paper or cramming for a final. She is frantically looking for every vital piece of information and needs my assistance to find everything she requires.

Some years ago, I worked at Carnegie-Mellon University. One of my tasks was to supervise undergraduate work-study students in one of the engineering departments. This experience gave me (in addition to the ulcers) an indelible picture of "Constance Reader." She's modeled after one of my student employees: outgoing, intelligent, eager, and naive as a lamb. One morning, she bounced into my office, her eyes as wide as saucers, totally amazed. When I asked her what was wrong, she replied, "You won't believe who I just saw walking across campus!"

I just grinned. Pittsburgh's most famous resident lives near the CMU campus. "You just bumped into Mr. Rogers, didn't you, dear?" Now, whenever I begin an undergraduate textbook, I remember the look of wide-eyed wonder on her face and know that I'm going to have to be *very* thorough.

In the Beginning

Usually, indexers receive textbook page proofs in chapter units, one or two at a time. The editor should also send the table of contents, which indicates which topics will be covered, and the prefatory material, in which the author discusses the thrust of the text—what point of view will be taken in *discussing* those topics.

If you do not automatically receive the following items, ask for them: index to (or copy of) the previous edition, any prefatory material, and the table of contents. If possible, find out what the author thought of the previous index. Examine the previous index—see if you can find any errors or inconsistencies, then make a note of them. Write down any questions you might have to ask the editor before you begin (it helps to have a questionnaire to fill out—see the sample worksheet in Appendix A). Then pick up chapter 2 and index it—get a feel for the author's rhythm. Note any problem areas. When you feel that you have made a careful preliminary evaluation, you should have a list of questions ready to ask the editor. Now, call and ask those questions. Put the answers you have written down in a file folder and keep it with the page proofs. Refer to it from time to time, especially if you have not worked on the project for a few days—it will refresh your memory. I often prepare a list of the major entries that appeared in the previous index, especially if the author liked it, because it tells me what he finds most important. I hang the list from a copy holder attached to my monitor, where I can glance at it easily and often.

History as Journalism

History is nothing more than yesterday's news. That is a simplification, but it provides us with a handy tool to attack a complex task. In "Introductory Journalism," I learned that the basics of every news story are the five Ws and an H: who, what, where, when, why, and how. When applied to a history text, the who, what, and where form the primary structure of its index. The when clarifies entries in the index, so that Constance Reader can find the why and how.

Name Dropping

I mark text fairly thoroughly before making entries, and the first things I mark are the names of people. They are easiest to find when the page is as yet untouched, and if a name is missed on the first pass, it will eventually be found on a subsequent pass, thus reducing the odds of omitting someone. Generally, all names mentioned in a history textbook are indexed—even those mentioned only in passing—because it is usually a publisher's (or author's) requirement.

I make it a practice to add an identifying subentry to each name entry.[1] The same person may be mentioned a number of times in a 600-800 page text, and the context of each reference can be important. It is impossible to predict on page 85 how many times the John Smith mentioned there will appear again in the next 600 pages, or whether fiendish impostors using the same name will show up to confuse us.

I use three references for biographical information: *Webster's New Biographical Dictionary* will answer the majority of questions. However, everyone listed in it is dead. So, I also use the *HarperCollins Dictionary of Biography*. It is not as complete but does list many living figures. Finally, my trusty old *Encyclopaedia Britannica* is the last place I look. If it's not there, I query the editor or author.

And Then There's Fred

There are four pages of Fredericks in *Webster's New Biographical Dictionary*: nine kings of Denmark; five electors of the Palatinate; four each of kings of Germany and grand dukes of Mecklenburg-Schwerin; three each of Holy Roman Emperors, kings of Prussia, kings of Sicily, rulers of Brandenburg, and electors of Saxony; plus a gaggle of miscellaneous princes, dukes, archdukes, lords, and so on. The mind boggles. Es-

---

1. I give you fair warning—the use of an "identifying subentry" is something I'm going to harp on throughout this article, because *it really works!*

pecially when you discover that "your" author has casually dropped Frederick Williams into the text without specifying which of seven rulers he's discussing!

We must be careful to label each Frederick accurately in the index. This may entail consulting the references mentioned above and may require inclusion of dates as well as titles. The result of my efforts might look like this:

Frederick William, Elector of Brandenburg (1640-1688)
Frederick William, Duke of Brunswick (1771-1815)
Frederick William I, Elector of Hesse-Kassel (1847-1866)
Frederick William I, King of Prussia (1713-1740)
Frederick William II, King of Prussia (1786-1797)
Frederick William III, King of Prussia (1797-1840)
Frederick William IV, King of Prussia (1840-1861)

You will notice that several of our Frederick Williams are geographically and temporally proximate. This makes it all the more important to identify the subject of discussion correctly.

Que Sera, Sera

One of the most difficult tasks in indexing history texts is to indicate the relationship of an historical event to its cause and results and to corollary events, without inserting repetitious subheadings or superfluous cross-references. We must direct the reader to a wide array of related (but not duplicated) information.

Part of that task is to consider the relative importance of the event. Let's use that trusty major historical event, war, as an example. A discussion of the Civil War in an American history text may result in a complex entry[2] such as:

Civil War, 381-408
    campaigns and battles of, 398-408. *See also individual battles and commanders*
    Confederate mobilization. *See* Confederacy
    economic issues in, 384. *See also* Cotton economy
    effect of westward expansion, 224
    historians' opinions on causes of, 384-385
    as moral conflict, 384
    Reconstruction and. *See* Reconstruction
    secession crisis and, 381-383
    slavery issue and. *See* Slavery; Slave Trade
    strategy and diplomacy, 395-398
    Union mobilization. *See* Union

You will notice that it is cross-referenced to such causative factors as slavery and economic issues that are major topics in and of themselves.[3]

---

2. A complex entry has two or more subentries and may include cross-references.

3. This concept works for any kind of complex entry in which the subentries discuss causation and results— it is not limited to wartime!

Regarding the battles, I have given a page range as well as a cross-reference. My rule of thumb is that if only one or two battles are discussed, I list them as individual subentries with page ranges. I would also provide simple entries[4] for each battle, including dates:

Chickamauga, Battle of (1863), 405

Gettysburg, Battle of (1863), 404-405

Conversely, if a number of battles are discussed, I provide simple entries as above, plus a page range and cross-reference as I did in the Civil War entry. If the battles are mentioned only in passing, and the references are scattered, the subentry would be:

Civil War
    battles of. See *individual battles and commanders*

Some indexers dislike cross-referencing from subentries, as I did in the Civil War example. I prefer it in textbooks because it provides the reader with information in the place she expects to find it. If her professor tells her to write about the battles of the Civil War, or about economic factors, she will look under Civil War for the specific subentries "battles" or "economic factors." We cannot assume that she will look at the end of a complex entry for a list of cross-references. And, if all cross-references for the Civil War entry above were placed at the end (or beginning) of the entry, imagine what it would look like:

Civil War
    See also Confederacy; Cotton economy; Reconstruction; Slavery;
    Slave trade; Union; *specific battles and commanders*

An Ongoing Problem

Information about a topic in a history text is not necessarily found, with a neat heading, in one place. Discussion of education, for example, may be scattered throughout the text within discussions of other main topics—colonial society, women, blacks, the radicalization of the 1960s, land grant institutions, and so on. How is the indexer expected to coordinate mentions of these various aspects of education into one useful complex entry?

Solution

Always add an explanatory subentry—then "flip" that entry into a second (or third) entry from another point of view. For example:

Colleges and universities, for women, 236

Education, of women, 236

Women, college education for, 236

On page 236, the discussion of college education for women might be a minor point. By page 426, it might be a subtopic of the general discussion of education in the United States. By page 726, it might be part of a discussion of the women's liberation movement or of the radicalization of college students.

---

4. A simple entry has no subentries and not more than 4-5 page locators.

"No Matter Where You Go, There You Are" (Buckaroo Banzai)

And you thought people and events could be confusing! What with wars and territorial acquisitions and shifting national boundaries (not to mention earthquakes and floods), it's a miracle that we know where we are! I couldn't get through a history text without my trusty *Webster's New Geographical Dictionary*. It provides alternative spellings, dates, brief histories, maps, and significant facts about each place, which is invaluable in resolving confusion.

At Home

An American history textbook should not have an entry for "United States." Each state mentioned should be indexed, however, with subheadings. Most states will end up with a simple entry and one or two locators, but some states, such as New York, Pennsylvania, and California, often wind up as complex entries. Since we cannot assume that Constance Reader was an ace in U.S. geography, cities mentioned should be indexed with the state indicated as:[5] "Chicago, Illinois" or "Chicago (Ill.)." The exception to this is New York, which is indexed as "New York City" as opposed to "New York State."

And Abroad

European (or world) history poses an entirely different set of problems. National boundaries that change over time can be very confusing to the indexer—imagine how confusing they are to the student! Let's look at Austria. At various times it has been (1) an archduchy, (2) under Spanish rule, (3) part of the Holy Roman Empire, and (4) part of Austria-Hungary. It has gained territory: Transylvania, Slavonia, Sardinia, Naples, and others. It has lost territory: Lombardy, Bohemia, Moravia, Galicia, and others. Thus, it is important for the indexer to add subentries with dates, to distinguish between something that happened in the Austria of 1512 and something that happened in the Austria (*Ostmark*) of 1942. If the indexer is not sure about an entry, the reader will be totally lost.

By Any Other Name

Similar place-names are another source of confusion. For example, a text may mention "Austrasia" in a discussion of Charlemagne. If the author is not scrupulously careful in identifying countries mentioned briefly, and the indexer is not careful in looking up unfamiliar names, the index might suggest that Charlemagne once ruled "Australia."

In order to prevent confusion in an index, use identifying subentries with each entry! Make sure that you distinguish between similar place-names, such as "Great Lake (Tasmania)" and "Great Lakes (U.S.)," or "Londonderry (England)" and "Londonderry (Northern Ireland)." It may seem tedious, but it prevents error and time lost in the editing process (when time is most precious) to go back and reexamine the text.[6]

---

5. Never use postal codes (IL, PA, etc.). If abbreviations are necessary, useful guides to correct usage are *Webster's New Geographical Dictionary* (pp. 14a-15a) and the *Chicago Manual of Style*.

6. By the time you are editing, the project deadline is looming large, you have probably scattered page proofs to the four winds, and what would have taken thirty seconds in the entering process now takes five minutes to find, check, and correct. Multiply that time by a mere twelve questions and you've lost an hour!

Place-name changes are an additional source of fun. Austria was known as Ostmark when it was occupied by Nazi Germany, and this might be mentioned in the text. Such cases can be handled in two ways. If the discussion of Ostmark is substantial, as it might be in a history of Nazi Germany, the main entry for "Ostmark (1938-1945)" could have as subentries those events that happened within that time period, plus a cross-reference, "*See also* Austria." On the other hand, a split entry is awkward and does not serve the reader well. In general texts, where mention of this would be minor, it is better to create the entry, "Ostmark (1938-1945). *See* Austria" and make the Ostmark information a subentry under Austria.

Slicing and Dicing

"OK, I've double- and triple-posted every possible entry. I've added explanatory subentries to everything that didn't move! This looks like a *swamp!* Now what do I do?"

Editing Made Easy

Editing is a process of evaluating what you have done, expanding on important concepts, and refining and polishing until the index shines as an elegant and useful part of the text. Then you have to make it fit into the number of pages the publisher gives you!

When you have finished making entries, spell-checking, verifying, and doing your on-screen cleanup, print out a double-spaced copy of the index (in formatted view). Put it on your desk. Go watch something really stupid on television. Get a good night's sleep, and don't look at that printout until the next day. If you have time to leave it there for two days, so much the better. When you pick up the printout and go to your comfy recliner to read it, I guarantee that a whole tribe of inconsistencies, errors, duplications, and omissions will jump out at you and yell, "*Boo!*"

Less Is More

I follow the rule of thumb that, in the finished index for a history textbook, if a main entry has less than five (5) page locators, it does not need subentries. The exception to that rule occurs when you must distinguish between two entirely different aspects of the main entry, as:

> Diplomatic recognition
> > of Latin American nations (1815)
> > of United States during Revolutionary War

In the above case, the concept of diplomatic recognition is less important than distinguishing which country is being recognized.

Snip, Snip

By this time, you will probably have a good mental picture of everything you've indexed. As you mark the printout for the unnecessary subentries you are going to delete, make notes in the margin to *search* for particular keywords that occur to you—you might wonder if you have all references to a large topic gathered correctly into a complex entry. You will see things you need to check in the text and entries you will need to combine with others or delete or cross-reference. Expect that your printout will look like a road map of Pittsburgh—red lines wandering everywhere on the page!

Now, take your marked printout to the computer and open your index file. *Do not delete anything!* Look through the printout for all markings of *search.* (If you eliminate the unneeded subentries before you search, you won't find anything.) At this point, you can either add information directly into the file or mark the additions on the printout. *Now* you can delete those pesky subentries!

Next, estimate the number of lines in the index and determine how much more you need to cut to have the index fit into the allotted page limits. (Aarrgghh!) Print out another copy of the index as before and repeat that good night's sleep—providing you have another day to make the final changes! Actually, the index should now look very good to you: complete, consistent, and useful. A touch of fine-tuning should do it, then a final spell-check and verification of cross-references, and you're ready to prepare your final package. All done—and on time.

Doing Splits

Occasionally, a textbook will be produced in two versions: the full text and "splits." Splits are either smaller versions of the original in which most of the chapters are the same but not all are included, or they are divided volumes for classes that cover two semesters. In either case, do not fear them, for you will be paid extra! All you need to do is index the main volume, then group the pages that will be used for the split(s) and save them *(unedited)* in a separate file. After you have completed the main index and sent it off, add whatever chapters you have received for the splits to that file and then repeat the editing process. The important thing to remember, whether you've made one or two additional files, is to edit each one separately as a stand-alone index. Normally, this process takes only a few days, but the publisher allows a minimum of a week. It's best to take a day or two "off" and rest before tackling the splits.

"Why?" (Nancy Kerrigan)

Few indexers do it only for the money, although taking that lovely check to the bank and making another payment on your new Mustang convertible is a powerful incentive to do a good job. In college, I majored in writing and minored in history, because I couldn't stop signing up for history courses—they fascinated me. The first time I found a famous ancestor in a text I was indexing, I called the editor just so I could tell someone about it. Lincoln's assassins were a major obsession throughout high school (OK, I attended a private school for girls and my social life was limited). I've read every book and seen every movie and documentary I could find on George Armstrong Custer, Jack the Ripper, and the Titanic.

Why do I like to index textbooks? Because they cover a wide range of information (Trivial Pursuiters, beware!), are logically organized, and have nice, firm beginning and ending dates that help me schedule other projects. Besides, once in a rare while, I get to correct an author! Last year I pointed out that "Mr. Smith (Jr.)" was as dead as a doornail—"It's Mr. Smith (III) who's the congressman." Delicious!

Appendix A: Project Worksheet

Title _____ Author _____

Publisher _____ Editor _____ Phone _____

Estimated total pages _____ Pages start _____ Pages end _____

Index due _____

Previous edition or index received? _____

Preface/Introduction/Table of Contents? _____

Number of book pages allotted for index(es) _____

Estimated number of entries per book page _____

Indented _____ or run-in _____ style?

Separate name index? _____

Bold-faced terms? _____

Figures and tables? _____

Boxed information or other special formats (preferred handling): _____

_____

Alphabetization: by letter _____ by word _____

How do you prefer that I note typos? _____

Questions/special instructions: _____

_____

_____

_____

Appendix B: General Indexing Procedure

1. Examine project thoroughly. Make notes and formulate questions for editor; prepare project folder for worksheet, cover sheets for batches of project, and any miscellaneous information from editor.
2. Index one sample chapter (*not* chapter 1) following item 6 below.
3. Formulate additional questions for editor; call editor and check all requirements; if you do not have them, ask for a copy of the publisher's guidelines for indexers. Fill out project worksheet.
4. Estimate number of pages that can be indexed per hour (total time for marking, entering, and editing) and determine work schedule for project—that is, the number of pages to be indexed per day (be sure to allow for any concurrent projects you are doing). *You have overestimated your pages-per-day output*—reduce estimate by 25 percent.[7]
5. As batches of proofs arrive, check them immediately: Mark cover sheet with date received, then count pages and check it against cover sheet. If there are missing pages, call the compositor and ask that they be sent with the next batch (you do not need to bother the editor with this).
6. Handle each chapter as a unit. I use this procedure because I work alone, and it allows me to switch tasks often to prevent tiredness and muscle cramps:
    a. Mark page proofs. Make several passes, highlighting names, bold-faced terms, and figures/tables in different colors.[8] This is the fastest way to be sure I can see and identify something instantly when I'm making entries. Mark page ranges of chapter headings and subheadings, including figures and tables.
    b. If a separate name (author) index is to be done, enter names. Separate author indexes are rarely done for history texts. At this point, I usually enter names and bold-faced terms into the subject index, for a break from marking.
    c. Read thoroughly, highlighting (I use yellow) all topics to be entered and marking page ranges for each. If any additional names are found, highlight them in a different color from that of the first pass. If you notice any typos, mark them as such and dog-ear a corner of the page.[9]
    d. Make entries for subject index. First, enter page ranges as marked for chapter headings and subheadings, making sure each is double-posted. Then enter finer points: color-coded items and yellow-highlighted topics. Create explanatory subentries for all main entries *except* bold-faced terms, which indicate definitions.
    e. Group together the entries for the chapter. Spell-check the group. While the chapter is fresh in your mind, examine main entries, *then* subentries, *then* page numbers for obvious errors, omissions, or anomalies. It requires concentration, but if you can train yourself to *look at one thing at a time,* you will pick up most inconsistencies immediately. Add any appropriate cross-references that may occur to you at this time.

---

7. "Everything takes longer and costs more" (anon.).
8. I use highlighters as follows: pink = people; orange = bold-faced terms; green = figures and tables. If necessary, I sometimes also use blue = places and purple = things (minor events, treaties, acts, amendments, etc.).
9. Normally, I return dog-eared pages to the editor with the index. Only if an error seems significant should you telephone the editor.

f. If the book is arranged into units, repeat the process in item e for each completed unit.
7. Editing the completed index:
    a. Spell-check and verify that cross-references are correct.
    b. View index in formatted layout—it is easier on the eyes if you double-space it. Read index from A to Z, *as if you were reading the text.* In this first pass, you will find the most obvious errors. Pay special attention to complex entries for subheads that can be combined and anything that suggests additional entries or cross-references.
    c. View index in page-number order to check for any page numbers out of correct range.
    d. Print out a copy of the index (double-spaced) and set it aside overnight.
    e. Read the printed copy thoroughly, marking any changes you wish to make. Less-obvious errors will show themselves at this point. Again, check for potential additions and cross-references. List in the margin any terms you might want to *search* the file for.
    f. If you have any further questions for the editor, now is the time to ask them. Double-check editor's requirements for disk submission and hard copy. Make sure you have used current indexer's guidelines from publisher.
    g. Make marked changes. If you have time, repeat items d and e. If you do not have time, repeat items a and b.
8. Make sure you have saved both index file (on hard drive) and backup file on floppy disk. Transfer index to publisher's preferred disk format and print out the final copy. It will save much time and grief if you have already tried this with a sample index in order to make sure that the publisher's preferred format will print properly without additional fluffing and buffing.
9. Package and send.[10]

Handy References for Your Bookshelf

The Annals of America. 1968. Chicago, Ill.: Encyclopaedia Britannica.
The Cambridge Factfinder. 1993. New York: Cambridge University Press.
Encyclopaedia Britannica. 1979, 1990. Chicago, Ill.: Encyclopaedia Britannica.
The HarperCollins Dictionary of Biography. 1993. New York: HarperCollins.
The Mosby Medical Encyclopedia. 1992. New York: Penguin.
The New York Public Library Book of Popular Americana. 1994. New York: Macmillan.
The New York Public Library Desk Reference. 1993. New York: Prentice-Hall.
Webster's New Geographical Dictionary. 1997. Springfield, Mass.: Merriam-Webster.
Webster's New Biographical Dictionary. 1988. Springfield, Mass.: Merriam-Webster.
Webster's New World Encyclopedia, Pocket Edition. 1993. New York: Prentice-Hall.

---

10. At this time, it may be appropriate to enjoy a little "whine" and cheese.

INDEXING ART AND ART HISTORY MATERIALS

Marilyn Rowland and Diane Brenner

Surprisingly, art and art history books, even those thick with details about artists and artwork, do not always have indexes. In fact, they often don't have indexes, or only cursory ones. Why is this? Well, according to some publishers, art books don't need indexes because the organization of the book, including tables of contents, chronologies, lists of illustrations, or glossaries, provides sufficient structure to allow readers to find what they are looking for. In other cases, the omission of the index may be a cost consideration or a lack of awareness of the importance of an index, even in a book consisting mainly of illustrations. Sometimes, even lengthy introductory discussions or historical essays are viewed as "too short" to bother indexing.

In those art and art history books that do have indexes, there is considerable variety in style and format. Sometimes this is because the indexer and the client have developed a style designed to meet the specific characteristics of the book. Sometimes it is because the indexer is not familiar with art history or aware of art history indexing conventions and does not know how to index art history materials effectively.

We hope, in this article, to provide some guidance on indexing books on art and art history: traditional art history textbooks, coffee-table art books, how-to books on art techniques, and books on related topics, such as crafts, architecture, design, photography, fashion, and, sometimes, archaeology and anthropology. Our goal is not to dictate rules to be applied in every situation but to provide the knowledge to know what questions to ask in each situation and where to go for important information.

Background Required (or Not Required)/ How to Get Work in This Field

A love of art and an interest in learning more about art are good qualities in art/art history indexers. If you enjoy art, indexing art and art history books can be a very satisfying specialization.

Although an art history degree will certainly help, you don't need to be an art historian to index art and art history materials. Clients are generally more interested in your skills as an indexer than your artistic credentials or knowledge. Most clients would like to see a familiarity with art and art history terms but do not require an art history degree.

Some clients may seek out an indexer with a degree in art history or a related field for a highly technical or academic text such as M. Spearman, editor of *The Age of Migrating Ideas: Early Medieval Art in Northern Britain and Ireland* (Edinburgh: National Museums of Scotland, 1992), or the Getty Museum's *Ancient Gems and Finger Rings: A Catalogue of the Collections* (Malibu: J. Paul Getty Museum, 1992). For an especially detailed book on painting techniques, it may help to know that the term "medium" specifically applies to the liquid part of paint. Thus, "oil paint" is not a medium, though the linseed oil in it is; similarly, the medium in tempera is egg yolk and that in watercolor or pastel is gum arabic. Likewise, the "ground" is the material on which a work of art is produced, for example, canvas, paper, or plastered wall. You may also need to be able to distinguish a Renaissance "cartoon" from a nineteenth-century "cartoon," and both from a "sketch," "study," or "caricature," or be aware that the word "grotesque" describes a type of Italian decoration that derived from Roman design. You may want to distinguish between "realism," "social realism," "surrealism," and "superrealism" and know how all these differ from "naturalism." And you should recognize that the word "value," as applied to color, means something quite different from the same word used in art criticism.

If you don't have an art history degree, you should take some time to become familiar with art styles and periods (e.g., impressionism, romanticism, futurism), significant artists (e.g., Michelangelo, Homer, Seurat, Hokusai), and basic art terms (e.g., abstraction, aesthetics, chiaroscuro, design, graphics, perspective). Reading through a good, general art history text (with a good index), such as H. W. Janson's *History of Art* (5th ed., New York: Harry Abrams, 1997); Sister Wendy Beckett's popular *Story of Painting: The Essential Guide to the History of Western Art* (London: Dorling Kindersley, 1994); Helen Gardner and colleagues' *Art Through the Ages* (10th ed., New York: Harcourt Brace, 1996); or E. H. Gombrich's *Story of Art* (New York: Phaidon, 1995), should give you a basic understanding of Western art traditions. Specialized books such as Richard M. Barnhart and colleagues' *Three Thousand Years of Chinese Painting* (New Haven, Conn.: Yale University Press, 1997), Robert Hughes' *American Visions: The Epic History of Art in America* (New York: Alfred Knopf, 1997), and Frederick Hartt and David G. Wilkins's *History of Italian Renaissance Art: Painting, Sculpture, Architecture* (New York: Harry Abrams, 1994) are typical of the type of titles you should look for if you want more in-depth knowledge. Visits to art museums, shows, and galleries are invaluable, as are introductory courses in art and art history, available at art museums, colleges, and community night schools.

Next, review the indexes in art and art history books. Look at the style and format of each index and how they differ from book to book (see below for more on this topic). Think about why the indexes might be different for different books. Are index formats and styles thoughtfully developed for each type of art book, or is there some indexer quirkiness at play? Look at the concepts indexed. Would you have selected similar entries and subentries? Are they entries that the typical art student or general reader might choose? Does the index anticipate the needs of the user?

Finally, especially if you are a new indexer, you may want to sit down and write a sample index for a book or a chapter in a book and compare it with the index in the back of the book. Learning by doing will give you a good understanding of the types of issues you may encounter in indexing art and art history materials. Resolve these questions before you go after your first job. Keep a list of stylistic and content questions so that you can ask your next art/art history client how she would like you to treat them in the work you do for her.

Begin your efforts to find work by compiling a list of potential clients who publish art and art history books. Include national publishers such as Harry Abrams, Harper-

Collins, George Braziller, Phaidon, Monacelli, and Lark Books, but look closer to home, too. You may find some small local publishers who are happy to work with a nearby indexer. Contact your local arts organizations, too, to see if they have any publications in the works that might need an index. If they do not have funds available to pay for an index, you might want to volunteer your services for a worthy cause. You'll gain experience in indexing art materials and a book to add to your résumé.

Instructions from the Client— What You Might Get and What You Might Need

Once you've convinced an editor you have the basic art history and indexing knowledge to do the job, you'll need instructions from the client on the particulars of the project. This task is complicated by the fact that many publishers do not have specific style guides for art and art history materials. You may be given some general indexing guidelines or simply told to follow the *Chicago Manual of Style*. All of the editors we spoke with have adopted the indexing guidelines in the 14th edition.

If no specific guidelines exist, ask for a copy of an index the editor or author felt was particularly well done or is a good example of an appropriate style and format. Ask specific questions. Should all works of art be posted twice: once under the name of the artwork and once under the name of the artist? Should locators for illustrations of artworks be in italics? Should artists' names be highlighted in some way? How should references to both a discussion of a piece of artwork and an illustration of that piece on the same page be treated? One reference in italics? One reference in bold? Two references, one in roman and one in italics? Ask if the author has a list of terms to be included in the index or if there is a glossary. Ask if there is an editor's style sheet that might be helpful in preparing the index. Ask about any space limitations.

Indexing Works of Art

In many types of materials, the indexer has the option of indexing illustrations or not, depending on whether they convey information in addition to the text on that page. In art and art history materials, however, it is usually important to index all illustrations and to differentiate between references to discussions of artwork and to illustrations of artwork. In many books on art history, references to works of art account for much of the total index.

Unless the client instructs you otherwise, index all artwork, both art discussed in the text and art shown in illustrations. Works of art are generally italicized and indexed both as main entries, with the name of the artist following in parentheses, and as subentries under the name of the artist. Locators referring to pages where artworks are illustrated are often italicized so the reader will know where to look to see a picture, rather than a discussion of the piece of art. Sometimes illustrations are referenced by plate or figure numbers.

Picasso, Pablo
    Mother and Child, 49, 93, 108
    Three Musicians, 47, *52*, 93

Mother and Child (Picasso), *49*, 93, 108
Three Musicians (Picasso), 47, *52*, 93

The exception to this rule is the case when artists and their cited works typically appear on the same page. Rather than list:

Monet, Claude, 705
   Impression, Sunrise, 705
   Iris, 705
   Plazzo da Mula, Venice, 705
   Poplars on the Epte, 705

it may be appropriate to list only:

Monet, Claude, 705

This is appropriate when all or most artists are discussed on a single page and might be especially useful if the space for the index is tight. It is a good idea to discuss this decision with the client.

If an artist has produced more than one work of art with the same title, include the date or dimensions of the work or other identifying information:

Degas, Edgar
   Rehearsal, The (1873-78), 45, *48*
   Rehearsal, The (1874), 45, *46*
   Rehearsal, The (1878-79), 45, *47*

You may also want to distinguish between color plates and other illustrations. There are various ways to do this. You might include in the locator the word color plate or use an abbreviation such as *clp.* or *CP.* Or you could use boldface or an asterisk. This notation can be put before or after the page number and may be put in parentheses. The following examples illustrate some of these methods:

Monet, Claude
   Houses of Parliament, Sunset, 842-43, *844,* **879**
   Impression—Sunrise, Le Havre, 844, *867 CP*
   Japanese Footbridge, The, 845, *870, 890**
   Rouen Cathedral in Full Sunlight, 723, 844, *clp 872,* 910
   Women in the Garden, 840, *875* (color plate)

It is best to talk to your client about what style to use and equally important to be consistent in the use of that style throughout the index.

Sometimes numbers are used to identify artwork throughout a book. In this case, it is sometimes helpful to include the illustration number in the locator. This, too, may be done in several ways. The illustration number could be in a different font or typography, listed as Roman numerals, or coded in some other way. In the example below, illustration number 600 appears on page 450.

Lawrence, Jacob
   Bread, Fish, Fruit, 450:*600*

In most books, it is not necessary to tell the reader whether a page includes both information on a topic and an illustration depicting the topic. In art and art history books, however, it may be important to do so:

Cassatt, Mary, 35-39
    Bath, The, 35, *35,* 39
    Family Group Reading, 36-38, *37*

If your index includes subentries about the artist, as well as subentries on his or her works, it may be appropriate to list subentries about the artist first, followed by artwork, rather than listing all subentries in alphabetical order:

Michelangelo Buonarroti, 23, 95, 176
    artistic philosophy, 25-26
    childhood, 24-25
    influence of, 39-40
    Creation of Adam, The, 42
    Last Judgment, The, 93, *97*

Works in a series are indicated by the word "series":

Waterlilies series (Monet), 34, *36*

Names of exhibitions are italicized and indicated by the word exhibition:

Hockney, David
    New American Painting, The (exhibition), 18, 258

Untitled works of art are indexed as *Untitled:*

Untitled (Judd), *43*

Not all works of art are traditional paintings or sculptures. Other forms of art may include architecture, furniture, photography, jewelry, textiles, and ceramics, contemporary, historical, ethnic, and folk crafts, prehistoric sculptures, sand paintings, cave paintings, and environmental art.

Works of architecture are not italicized, but the architect's name is included in parentheses and distinguishing information may be given:

Kimbell Art Museum, Fort Worth (Kahn), 433, *434*

Sometimes the index provides information about the materials or type of art:

colossal head, Olmec, 129
Leopard (ivory*), 278*
Olmec head (basalt), *129*
Wounded Bison Attacking a Man (cave painting), 88

Named craft pieces are italicized, while unnamed, anonymous, or generic artworks generally are not. However, the author may choose to italicize all the names of all works of art, even if they are just descriptive: as in *Wounded Bison Attacking a Man,* above, a descriptive, yet italicized name. Follow the italicization in the text.

adornment
    beaded hoops, 26
    Hausa robe of honor, 3033
    Ndebele beaded apron, 2629

Foreign words are often italicized, though commonly known terms may not be:

calabash, 134, 167. *See also elletel; kakool*
gungulu (armlets), 121, 142
liagi (Fulani amulet), 153

However, italicization of foreign terms or technical phrases is often highly idiosyncratic. In E. H. Gombrich's classic *Story of Art*, all technical terms are italicized, whether or not they derive from a foreign language:

Block-books, 203
Chiaroscuro, 18
Choir, 92

and in Mary Gostelow's equally classic *Embroidery*, it appears that italics are reserved for foreign items of clothing, but not other foreign terms, though there is no note of explanation:

Shikara, 238
Shisha stitch
Shor, 147
Shu-ching, 250

The lesson here seems to be that it's best to get such matters clear, either by consulting with your editor or developing your own consistent approach, and to let the reader know in an explanatory note the meaning of special typography used in your index (see below).

Indexing Names

Most of the rules governing indexing the names of artists and other people mentioned in art and art history books are not unique to the field of art and art history. Guidelines for indexing names can be found in the *Chicago Manual of Style* and books on indexing, such as Nancy Mulvany's *Indexing Books* and Hans Wellisch's *Indexing from A to Z*. A good biographical dictionary is indispensable.

Be alert to indexing and alphabetizing conventions for foreign names, married women's names, pseudonyms, variants in spelling and form, prefixes, and related issues. For example, both "Brueghel, Pieter, the Elder" and "Bruegel, Pieter, the Elder" are acceptable spellings (sometimes found in the same book). You might want to put both as in "Brueghel (Bruegel), Pieter, the Elder." Also correct are both "Van Dyke, Sir Anthony" and "Vandyke, Sir Anthony."

Use full or commonly known names in the index: "Rembrandt" or "Rembrandt Harmenszoon van Rijn" (or Ryn), *not* "van Rijn, Rembrandt." Other examples include "El

Greco (Domenicos Theotocopoulos)" and "Michelangelo" or "Michelangelo Buonarroti," *not* "Buonarroti, Michelangelo."

Alphabetization is sometimes tricky. Most indexers know that Von and Van are usually ignored in alphabetizing. Knowing that rule, but believing all rules have exceptions, Marilyn alphabetized Vincent Van Gogh under "Van" because people refer to him as Van Gogh. Had she looked in *Webster's New Biographical Dictionary*, a standard reference source for indexers, she would have found Van Gogh listed in the G's.

Because other indexers have indexed Van Gogh under V, and because some readers might also look under G, especially in a book for the general public, Marilyn might have included a *See* reference to Gogh under V, thus educating others in the process. The moral to this story is: if you are not certain, look it up! There are many good print and online reference sources that can be of help. Every indexer should have a good biographical dictionary. Indexers who hope to specialize in art and art history should invest in one or more good dictionaries of art and artists (see the reference list at the end of this article for some suggestions).

There are also many free and subscription sources of information on the Web. One particularly good free online source is the Getty Information Institute's Union List of Artist Names Browser (http://www.gii.getty.edu/ulan_browser/).

Marilyn indexed a book on women artists in 1996, in which Berenice Abbott was referred to both as Berenice and Bernice. She could not find her listed in any of her sources and queried the editor about the spelling. Now, in 1998, she very easily and quickly found Berenice Abbott in the Union List of Artist Names Browser, along with biographical information indicating that she is the same person mentioned in the book. Marilyn would still note the discrepancy to the editor, but she would have been able to provide the editor with the correct spelling. With her art history background and personal connections, Diane would not have had to check any sources. She has personally met Berenice Abbott and has a signed photo of hers.

In this same index, Marilyn had queried another name, Properzia di Rossi, because she was referred to by her full name several times, rather than only her last name like all other artists in the book. Marilyn was uncertain whether to put her under P or R. Using the Union List, she found nothing under di Rossi. Then she searched on Properzia and found Rossi, Properzia de'. Marilyn now knew how to alphabetize the name and also found a spelling variant or error in the text, which she would have queried.

Don't feel that you must avoid querying the editor. Sometimes it is the only way to find the answer or to call the editor's attention to a possible error. When you have a question regarding spelling, alphabetization, whether to index Madeline Landing Pots under L or P, or whether

> Kelley, Walter
> Kelly, W.
> Kelly, Walt
> Kelly, Walter

are all the same person (unless you are absolutely sure from the context), query the editor.

Indexing Concepts

Concepts to be indexed in art and art history books will, of course, vary depending on the type of book and subject matter. In general, however, include historical periods, styles, technologies, materials, and historical context.

If you plan on indexing art and art history materials, invest in one or more of the art history reference books listed at the end of this article. Familiarize yourself with important periods, materials, and terms.

In general, art history indexes should include (at least) *movements* (e.g., fauvism, impressionism, classicism, dadaism), *styles* (e.g., Ionic, rococo, craftsman, Romanesque), *important techniques* (e.g., fresco, intaglio, mosaic, post and beam), *relevant geographic regions* (e.g., Egypt, Greece, Rome, Florence, China), *relevant time periods* (e.g., Neolithic, postindustrial, postmodern, Ming dynasty, Louis Quatorze, colonial America), and *relevant historical events* and *cultures* (e.g., French Revolution, Vikings, Incas, Yoruba).

Arts and crafts how-to book indexes should include *materials* (paper, brushes, gouache), *equipment* (light meter, inkle loom), and *techniques* (overpainting, diamond eyelet stitch, *cire perdue* [lost wax] casting), and *terms* (contour, glaze, foreground, hue, texture).

Sometimes the focus of a book is not clear or does not readily lend itself to indexing. Diane indexed a book that was simultaneously a book about seventeenth- and early eighteenth-century barns and an autobiography about a man who saves and restores them, authored by the barn-saver and a cowriter. Since so much of the history was presented as quotes from the author's "Gramps," with explanatory historical material interspersed with reminiscences and tales of roofs falling in, deciding on the focus and how to present the biographical versus the historical components became quite a challenge. Diane finally decided to treat the work as a biography, viewing the author in the third person.

As in other indexing projects, keep the reader's interests in mind when you choose your terms and be aware of synonyms and related terms, using *See* and *See also* references to tie related terms together.

Explanatory Notes

Be sure to include an explanatory note at the beginning of an index if you have used special typography—italics, bold, or other coding—so that your system is clear to the reader. For example, the introductory note for Frederick Hartt's *Art History of Painting, Sculpture, and Architecture* (New York: Harry Abrams, 1976) reads: "Page numbers are in roman type. Figure numbers of black-and-white illustrations are in *italic* type. Colorplates are denoted with an asterisk.* Names of artists and architects whose works are illustrated are in CAPITALS."

Appendix: Thesauri as Information Sources
by Diane Brenner and Alison Chipman

A good thesaurus has two main functions: it presents terms and concepts within an easily viewable hierarchical structure, and it provides, for any given term or concept, all the different terms and spellings used to express it. This can act like a "topographical map," providing an overall view of a concept or can act like a "road map," providing various routes to get to that concept.

For the indexer of art and art history books, an art and architecture thesaurus such as the one available through the Getty Information Institute (http://www.gii.getty. edu/aat_browser) can provide both a quick overview of a topic and can help identify important interrelationships among topics that may be scattered throughout a text or, perhaps, not directly stated. For instance, a discussion about Frank Lloyd Wright might touch on the low-cost housing designs he termed "Usonian houses," though the author might not discuss affordable housing per se. Nonetheless, it would be helpful to have "affordable housing. *See* Usonian houses" as a cross-reference in the index. A thesaurus can help an indexer, especially someone who is not fully conversant in a subject area, identify such access points.

Thesauri are especially useful when indexing collected works where different authors may use different terms to describe similar concepts. An art and architecture thesaurus is different from an encyclopedia or dictionary in that it shows the connections that exist among concepts independent of any one author's perspective. Moreover, it presents information at a glance, in a very concise form. In addition to a "hierarchical listing" that puts a term within a broad context, there is a "scope note" stating precisely (one hopes) what the concept is, and a list of all the terms that are used to represent that concept. An indexer would have to take the time to read carefully through a lengthy entry in a multivolume encyclopedia of art to get the same information about the content of a term, as well as various ways that term might be expressed and spelled. For indexers, when time is critical, a thesaurus provides an important ready reference.

As an example, if an indexer were indexing a book on appliqué needlework, a search of the browser site listed above would produce:

Processes and Techniques Hierarchy

<textile processes and techniques>
  <textile working processes and techniques>
    <needleworking and needleworking techniques>
      needleworking
        appliqué
            broderie perse
            reverse appliqué
        beading
        embroidering
        needlepoint
        piecing
        quilting
        whitework

This might alert her to some related areas of needlework to look out for in the text. It also informs her about two major subtypes of appliqué: "broderie perse" and "reverse appliqué." If, further, the indexer turns to the scope notes, she finds appliqué defined as the "technique of forming a design by applying cut out pieces of a material to a ground material; generally associated with needleworking but also used in ceramics, leatherworking, woodworking and metalworking." In addition, she would learn that in England, appliqué is called "applied work" and that other terms for appliqué that she might want to include in the index are "laid work," "laid on work," "work, laid on," and "onlay process." The indexer would also be referred to the related concepts of "on-lays" and "patchwork" that, in turn, might provide additional terms for synonyms or cross-references. Going to the associated subheadings, one level deeper, the scope notes on "broderie perse" would identify it as "an 18th century form of appliqué in which motifs such as flowers and animals are cut from cotton textiles, especially chintz, and stitched to a plain ground" and provide numerous other synonyms, including "cretonne work, Persian embroidery, [and] cut-out chintz appliqué." All this information is available both quickly and concisely.

An art and architecture thesaurus deals with terms from an historical perspective and can allow indexers to make material accessible to modern audiences by linking obsolete or passé terms to current common usage. For example, in zoo architecture, "elephant pavilions" became "pachyderm houses" that then became the current "elephant houses." The term "art deco" has gone through numerous permutations including "moderne," "art moderne," "jazz modern," "American deco," "art décoratif," and "style moderne."

Besides currency, there is the matter of terms borrowed by English speakers and writers from other languages. This happens frequently in the literature of art and art history, and here a thesaurus can be invaluable in keeping track of the many different spellings that can arise when a word from one language is transliterated into another. For instance, the term "ushabti," for the figures of servants placed in ancient Egyptian tombs to serve the deceased in the afterlife, is also spelled "shabti," "shawabti," "ushabtis," and "ushabtiu." The term "Kwere," used to designate the style of art and material culture produced by the Tanzanian ethnic group of the same name also occurs as "Bakwere," "Kwele," "Oukwere," and "Wakwere." The string instrument "citterns" also occurs as "ceteras," "cisters," "cistres," "citherns," "cithrens," and "citthorns."

Indexers can find a wealth of information in a good thesaurus—information that fosters better understanding of the materials they work on, thus helping create better indexes.

Acknowledgments

Special thanks to Sheila Samson, vice-president of Editorial Services, Guild Press of Indiana (http://www.guildpress.com), for her helpful comments. Thanks also to Alison Chipman of the Getty Institute's Art and Architecture Thesaurus, for providing the first draft of the appendix on thesauri.

Print Resources

A good general dictionary and biographical dictionary may provide all the information an art/art history indexer needs to produce an excellent index. Reference compendiums, such as *The New York Public Library Desk Reference*, also contain helpful sections. However, for those who seek more specialized tools the following dictionaries and encyclopedias might prove useful (as well as provide interesting reading).

General References

Chilvers, Ian, ed. 1997. *The Concise Oxford Dictionary of Art and Artists*. Oxford: Oxford University Press.

Chilvers, Ian, Harold Osborne, and Dennis Farr, eds. 1994. *The Oxford Dictionary of Art*. Oxford: Oxford University Press. A dictionary of international museums and galleries with more than 3,000 entries on Western painting, sculpture, drawing, graphic arts, and applied arts, treating artists, schools, periods, techniques, critical terms, and more.

Diamond, David, ed. 1992. *The Bulfinch Pocket Dictionary of Art Terms*. Boston: Little, Brown. It includes concise definitions for over 900 terms, drawings describing architectural elements, and a bibliography.

Mayer, Ralph. 1995. *Dictionary of Art Terms and Techniques*. New York: HarperCollins. It covers all forms of easel and mural painting, drawing, sculpture, graphic arts, photography, ceramics and mosaics; contains over 3,200 well-defined terms encountered in the study and practice of visual arts, including schools, styles, and periods; 100 line drawings.

Murray, Peter, and Linda Murray. 1992. *Penguin Dictionary of Art and Artists*. New York: Penguin. Simply a classic.

Ocvirk, Otto, Robert Stimson, Philip Wigg, Robert Bone, and David Cayton.1994. *Art Fundamentals, Theory and Practice*. Dubuque, Ia.: W. C. Brown. An extremely helpful and profusely illustrated introduction to art terminology.

Smith, James. 1998. *From Abacus to Zeus: A Handbook of Art History*. Englewood Cliffs, N.J.: Prentice-Hall. Designed as a comprehensive supplement to Janson, *History of Art* (5th ed.); Hartt, *Art* (4th ed.); and Gardner's *Art Through the Ages* (9th ed.), but also appropriate as a stand-alone brief reference test. This handbook defines the most common terms used in discussing the history of visual arts.

West, Shearer, ed. 1996. *The Bulfinch Guide to Art History: A Comprehensive Survey and Dictionary of Western Art and Architecture*: Bulfinch Press. First published in the U.K. as *The Bloomsbury Guide to Art*, the first North American edition is a worthy complement, and in some ways successor, to *The Oxford Companion to Art* (1970) and *The Oxford Dictionary of Art* (1988). This edition both updates the Oxford titles and offers features they lack such as art historical essays and plates containing 187 reproductions. The dictionary section covers some topics that the Oxford texts do not. For example, the Oxford Companion has no entry for Frida Kahlo or Diego Rivera. While the focus is Eurocentric, there are articles on Aboriginal art,

Chinese art, Mandala, and Hokusai. Entries range from a few sentences to more than a page.

More Specific References

Atkins, Robert. 1997. *Art Speak: A Guide to Contemporary Ideas, Movements and Buzzwords, 1945 to Present* (Speak Series). New York: Abbeville Press. Nearly 120 entries that clearly explain the who, what, where, and when of American and European art since 1945.

Carr-Gomm, Sarah. 1995. *Dictionary of Symbols in Western Art.* New York: Facts on File. An introduction to the meaning of symbols in Western art; visual themes, religious and mythological, that occur in figurative paintings and sculpture from the late Middle Ages to the nineteenth century.

Hall, James, with Chris Puleston (illustrator). 1996. *Illustrated Dictionary of Symbols in Eastern and Western Art.* New York: HarperCollins. A companion volume to the author's perennial seller *The Dictionary of Subjects and Symbols in Art*, this useful guide explains the meanings of the symbols used in the art of Egypt, the ancient Near East, Christian and classical Europe, India, and the Far East.

Julier, Guy. 1993. *The Thames and Hudson Encyclopedia of 20th Century Design and Designers.* New York: Thames and Hudson.

Murray, Peter, and Linda Murray. 1996. *The Oxford Companion to Christian Art and Architecture.* Oxford: Oxford University Press. Over 1,700 alphabetical entries that cover everything from Adam and Eve and the good Samaritan to illuminated books and rose windows; 200 illustrations, 16 color plates.

Pile, John F. 1994. *Dictionary of 20th Century Design.* New York: DaCapo. Some 1,200 alphabetical entries that define, identify, and explain names, terms, and concepts important to twentieth-century design; includes 200 black-and-white illustrations.

And . . . If You Really Get into This Field

Groves *Dictionary of Art* (1996), a 34-volume compendium with 41,000 articles from 6,700 contributors from 120 countries, plus 15,000 illustrations and 720,000 separate entries.

Web Resources

If you want to find art or art history sites on the Internet or if you want to find information about a specific subject, all you have to do is load one of the search engines (Alta Vista, Excite, Lycos, Yahoo) and type the words you want to search (e.g., "art history") in the space provided. To help you sort through the possibly thousands of responses you might get, here are a few sites we found especially helpful.

Art and Art History References and Links
http://www.marisol.com/maasi/art.htm
An online appendix to this article containing up-to-date Web site link and references.

Voice of the Shuttle (Alan Liu)
http://humanitas.ucsb.edu/shuttle/art.html#general-art

A truly vast, thorough, and current listing from the University of California at Santa Barbara of virtually everything relevant to art and art history with side links to similarly detailed pages on archaeology, architecture, and photography.

Art on the Web (Jeff Howe)
http://www.bc.edu/bc_org/avp/cas/fnart/artweb_links.html
Another vast, current list, produced at Boston College. A bit more of an art history education focus, with emphasis on "visual literacy."

History of Art Virtual Library
http://www.hart.bbk.ac.uk/VirtualLibrary.html
This comes from Birkbeck College at the University of London and has a broad European focus. Side links into the Museums Virtual Library and the Architecture Virtual Library.

Art History Resources on the Web (Chris Witcombe)
http://witcombe.bcpw.sbc.edu/ARTHLinks.html
Yet another detailed list of art history resources, by time periods, compiled by a professor of art history in the department of art history at Sweet Briar College, Virginia.

National Museum of American Art
http://www.nmaa.si.edu/
A great source of information on American art, including a useful reference section and an opportunity to ask questions.

The Art and Architecture Thesaurus (*see also* appendix)
http://www.gii.getty.edu/aat_browser/
The AAT is a controlled vocabulary for describing and retrieving information on fine art, architecture, decorative art, and material culture.

The Union List of Artist Names
http://www.gii.getty.edu/ulan_browser/
The ULAN is a database of biographical and bibliographical information on artists and architects, including a wealth of variant names, pseudonyms, and language variants.

And don't forget one of the best all-purpose resources:

The Library of Congress
http://lcweb.loc.gov/
The Library of Congress has a vast collection of American art and photography, as well as a search engine that lets you find books in their collection by subject as well as author, title, and so on. Everything about everything and a great way to check titles and names.

A PLACE IN THE INDEX:
GENDER AND SEXUAL ORIENTATION AS ISSUES IN INDEXING HISTORY

Victoria Baker

As indexers, our job is to bring forward the worldview presented in a book, adding value by giving another perspective on the book, as well as creating a repository of the facts. It is important to be able to understand the author's point of view and to possess the language skills to express it. It is essential not to introduce one's own prejudices into an index. It is also necessary to enlarge the context of the book, to anticipate language and perspective, in order to draw in the reader who is not already privy to the author's point of view. We all do this as we write cross-references from synonyms that are not used in the text to the terms that are (Mulvany 1994, 8, 12, 101).

Another aspect of the task of drawing in the reader involves choosing language for complex social issues. I will discuss gender and sexual-orientation issues in indexing. I consider this work to be a point of departure for further investigation, not the "truth" for all time. I am writing about my own practice as it has developed through schooling, reference works, and experience. For clarity, my examples are given in the indented style, regardless of the published format.

Flexibility of Term Choice

I wish to stress that as I discuss term choice I am referring to texts in which the author has used several terms for the same concept. This is the point at which the indexer has flexibility in term choice. If, however, the author has used only one particular term for a concept, the indexer is generally constrained to use that term. In this event, it is good indexing practice to write cross-references from current best usage, as well as from other synonyms, to the actual term used (Mulvany 1994, 8, 12). For example, if the author has used the terms "homosexuals" or "homosexuality" exclusively (not currently considered the best usage), one would cross-reference thusly:

> gay men. *See* homosexuals
> lesbians. *See* homosexuals

Indexers must stay abreast of language changes in our fields; we who index in social fields must also stay in touch with language changes regarding complex social issues.

Organizational Concepts

There are three concepts that underlie my word choice and overall organization of indexes involving complex social issues: sensitivity to labels, specificity, and point of view. "Sensitivity to labels" involves calling people what they prefer to be called, while understanding that these preferences are not universal and that they change over time (APA 1994, 48). It also means that we recognize the ways in which nonparallel labeling creates bias. The classic example of this is the phrase "man and wife," which defines the woman only in relation to her husband. "Husband and wife" or "man and woman" are parallel labels (APA 1994, 48-49; Miller and Swift 1988, 102-3; Judd 1990, 140).

"Specificity" involves choosing terms that are precise, but only as precise as the text warrants. As indexers are aware, the level of detail of the text on a given subject generally determines the level of detail in the index. So, too, are there multiple levels possible when dealing with gender or sexual orientation as a part of a book.

"Point of view," in relation to complex social issues, also helps determine term choice and index organization. I'll refer back to these three concepts as I give examples.

Gender

I think most of us agree it would be nice if gender wasn't such an issue, and, very naturally, indexers seem to avoid the issue if at all possible. Nevertheless, we find that our indexes contain main headings for women and frequently do not contain main headings for men. Why? Very simply, many books are written from the point of view that men are the norm and women are the departure from the norm. Thus, we accumulate specific subentries about women, while the background context, essentially unindexable, is about men. Conversely, books written specifically about women are sometimes indexed as if men were the primary context, that is, the point of view is ignored. I've developed some strategies for addressing these problems, but first let's define some terms and address some concerns about overcoming bias in language.

Definitions

Gender is a product of culture. Most cultures differentiate between males and females, but cultures vary widely as to what is expected from the role of woman or man. The terms "gender," "women," and "men" should be used for social/cultural concerns. The term "sex," on the other hand, refers to biology. The terms "sex," "female," and "male" should be used when biology is the primary concern.[1] Because "sex" can be confused with sexual behavior, I sometimes use "sex (biological)" as my term. (It is sometimes difficult to draw these distinctions, because environment and biology interact biochemically.) "Sexual dimorphism" refers only to physical sex differences and not to hormonal or other differences, so it is a less encompassing term.

---

1. The *American Heritage Dictionary* (3d ed.) gives a usage note on "gender" that supports this distinction between gender and sex. The distinction is now more widespread than that dictionary acknowledges and is common in scholarly works and textbooks. Nonetheless, inconsistencies do appear; thus the rule to assist indexers as we encounter them. Note, too, that the meaning of "gender" as used to refer to human beings is a later construct; its original, still-active meaning as a grammatical category is held by some linguists to be the only legitimate usage. *See also* the quote (Miller and Swift 1988, 8) under the text heading, "Overcoming Language Biases."

Thus, the terms "gender differences" and "sex differences" refer to cultural and biological differences, respectively. "Gender roles" may also be useful as the gathering point. Gender role is the role a person is expected to play as a result of being female or male in a particular culture. The term *gender role* is gradually replacing the term *sex role,* because sex role continues to suggest a connection between biological sex and behavior (Strong and DeVault 1997, 122). There are many other gender-related terms, such as "gender role stereotypes" (a further breakdown of gender-role analysis), but usually the text itself will define the terms if deeper analysis is warranted.

Overcoming Language Biases: Why? Is It an Agenda?

The point of all of this is to acknowledge the socially determined nature of gender, thereby ameliorating the gender imperative, which is biased in favor of men. Terms such as gender, gender differences, or gender roles help neutralize a traditional bias, a bias that alienates readers. Casey Miller and Kate Swift state, "To go on using in its former sense a word whose meaning has changed is counterproductive. The point is not that we *should* recognize semantic change, but that in order to be precise, in order to be understood, we must" (1988, 8).

Again, that we choose our language carefully makes the index more inclusive, thereby making the text more accessible. A core definition of the indexer's job is to make the text accessible (Mulvany 1994, 4). Attention to language and inclusivity does not constitute an agenda of the indexer, as is sometimes thought, but rather it constitutes the very essence of our work.

Men as Norm

When I find that I have an entry for women but not for men, I reanalyze the subentries. I look for evidence that the subentries for women are in actuality a comparison of the ways in which the roles and experiences of women and men differ. I place these subentries at a main heading related to gender, such as "gender differences." Frequently, this eliminates the entry for women. I then place the cross-references thusly:

> men. *See* gender differences
> women. *See* gender differences

If the entry for women still has subentries that are solely about women, I place the cross-references thusly:

> gender differences
>   [*subentries . . .*]
>   *See also* women
> men. *See* gender differences; women
> women
>   [*subentries . . .*]
>   *See also* gender differences

I am always careful to make the cross-reference from a main heading for men. The fact of the absence of subentries at men and the cross-reference to women helps alert the reader that the point of view assumes men to be the primary context. This is, of course, remaining true to the point of view of the book, but takes the additional step of helping to clarify the book's point of view. This step is frequently taken for granted for minority standpoints but is less frequently recognized as necessary for majority or male-as-norm points of view.

If I have collected some subentries under men, I also look at those closely, hoping to consolidate the subentries under "gender differences." One clue about whether subentries can be moved to a "gender" entry is if there are similar subentries under both "men" and "women." Another clue, of course, is when gender itself is explicitly discussed. If I still have an entry for men, with locators, I add "men" to the *See also* references under "women" and "gender differences." However, depending on the text, I sometimes write cross-references from "men" or "women" to the "gender" main heading only, underscoring the source of difference:

> gender
>   See also men; women
> men
>   See also gender
> women
>   See also gender

I follow the same strategies with "females," "males," and "sex differences" or "sex (biological)."

Women as Point of View

I mentioned that sometimes a book about women is still indexed as though men were the context and women the exception. Paradoxically, an index that stays inside the point of view of women frequently produces an entry for women, even as an entry for men accrues (unlike the situation for the male-as-norm point of view). I believe this is because we still have difficulty, as a culture, treating women as the norm. Although this is changing, we write books *about* women, as opposed to books with a worldview that everything is about women unless stated otherwise. One of the ways I ensure that women remain the focus is to make sure my subentries reflect this focus. Compare these two entries:

> Senecas
>   women as viewed by
> Senecas
>   women in society of

The first subentry assumes that Seneca society is male, viewing and defining women. The second assumes that society is a larger entity, composed of both men and women. Obviously, I believe the second is the accurate (specific) subentry.

Another signpost that I'm indexing from the author's point of view, in this case focused on women, is to look at the nature of the subentries under "women" and "men."

If the entry for "women," as opposed to that for "men," looks like the entry for the main subject of any book, then the focus is correct. In the following example, the entry for "women" consists of some subentries with locators and quite a few *See* references, as opposed to the entry for "men," which contains more subentries with locators (since the instances are more discrete). Compare these partial, representative entries from a text on the psychology of women (Donelson 1998):

men
    adjustment of, 96-98
    ageing and, 487-488, 494, 502
    aggression and. *See* aggression; violence
    alcohol and. *See* alcohol, use and abuse of
    anger and. *See* anger\
    anxiety and, 580-581
    battering and, 544-550
    biology and. *See* males
    child sexual abuse and, 539-541
    as comparison group, 29-30
    depression and, 568-569, 573, 576
    disadvantages for being, 81-82, 609
    empathy and, 311
    as feminists, 13-14, 17, 27
    hysterectomy and, 501
    infant interaction with, 136, 137
    leadership and, 305-308
    ludic behavior of, 346
    menstruation and, 191, 205, 208
    as norm. *See* male as norm
    women compared to. *See* gender differences
    [*and so on*]
women
    as abnormal, 216-217, 394, 499. *See also* male as norm
    achievement motivation and. *See* achievement motivation
    adjustment of, 96-97
    adolescent. *See* adolescents
    agentic traits and. *See* agentic traits and behaviors
    ageing and. *See* ageing
    AIDS and, 380-381, 382-384
    alcohol and. *See* alcohol, use and abuse of
    anxiety and. *See* anxiety
    battered, 544-550
    biology and. *See* females
    childless, 425-427
    cognitive abilities of. *See* cognitive abilities
    communal traits and. *See* communal traits and behaviors

eating disorders, 100-101, 181, 583-590, 591
employment and. *See* employment
family and. *See* families
in groups. *See* group dynamics
infant interactions with, 136-140
infertile, 427
language and. *See* communication; language
male as norm for. *See* male as norm
men compared to. *See* gender differences
[*and so on*]

Balance

Early attempts to bring women into history resulted in separate chapters or sections titled "Women." This was glaring evidence of the women-as-exception rule. Now, however, books are being written that balance the traditional bias, texts in which both men and women are treated as actors in society, even when the subject is a historical period in which women were considered chattel or the wards of men (which of course would include virtually all of Western history before the twentieth century). Following are the entries for "women," "men," and "gender roles" from a history of ancient Greece (Martin 1996). Despite the integration of women throughout the book, the entry for women is much larger than that for men, again a reflection of the fact of women having been conceptualized, throughout Western history, as the exception to the male norm. [Note that some of the *See also* references in this example were written by me as *See* references; the editor rewrote them for publication.]

gender roles
Aristotle on, 184
Cynics on, 215
inequalities, sources of, 7, 12-13, 20 . . .
labor specialization and, 6-7, 12-13
and patriarchy, rise of, 20
Plato's utopia and, 181
Stoics on, 214
the tragedies and, 133-134
See also men; women
men
in agricultural societies, 12-13
as colonists, 56
of Dark Age, 44-45, 48
in hunter-gatherer societies, 7
inequality among, 61, 79
marketing for household, 66
representations of, in art, 122, 123
sexual rights of, 66, 69, 78 . . .

Spartan training, 77-78, 79
sports and, 46-47
See also citizenship; democracy; gender roles; marriage; warrior
    societies
women
    abandonment of infants, 207-208
    in agricultural societies, 12
    Alexander the Great's treatment of, 193
    Aristotle on, 136, 183, 184
    as artists, 211
    of Athens, 135-139, 166-167
    citizenship of, 53, 61-62, 69
    as colonists' wives, 56
    duties of, 45, 67-69, 78-79 . . .
    education of, 140, 208, 212, 213
    elite, 45, 67, 125 . . .
    of Hellenistic period, 199, 206-208 . . .
    homosexuality of, 89, 141
    in hunter-gatherer societies, 6-7
    kidnapping of, 20, 56, 61
    male guardians required for, 61, 68-69, 136 . . .
    medicine and, 183, 217
    modesty expected of, 137-138, 139
    pallor of, 137-138
    philosophical schools welcoming, 181, 213, 214 . . .
    Plato's utopia and, 181
    as poets, 89, 90, 210-211
    poor, 68, 125 . . .
    property and inheritance rights of, 61, 68, 79 . . .
    as prostitutes, 67, 69, 139 . . .
    religion and, 59-60, 61-62, 68 . . .
    representations of, in artforms, 122, 123 . . .
    sexuality and, 66, 69, 79 . . .
    as slaves, 66, 139
    Socrates and, 166-167, 171, 181
    of Sparta, 68, 78-79, 136 . . .
    sports and, 46, 47, 68 . . .
    as theater attendees, 134, 164
    warfare and, 104, 105, 163 . . .
    See also childbearing; gender roles; marriage

Here is another example, taken from an anthropology of the Lakota Sioux sweat lodge ceremony (Bucko 1998):

gender
    as an issue, 237
    dialectic of tradition and, 40
    group focus and, 234, 256
    inclusiveness of, 2-3, 53, 205
    segregation by, 80, 181, 205
men
    dressing for ceremony, 11
    dress of, 3
    location of, in lodge, 3
    See also gender
women
    coming of age ceremony, 36, 287 n.18
    contemporary accounts of, 65
    dressing for ceremony, 11
    dress of, 2-3
    ethnohistoric accounts of, 35, 40
    interpretations and, variation in, 212
    location of, in lodge, 3
    menstruation, 36, 202, 205 . . .
    rebirth symbolism and, 205
    segregation of, 80, 181, 205
    sweats for, 207-209
    See also gender

Please note that many of the subentries under the "men" and "women" main headings in each of the indexes quoted above could have been consolidated under a "gender differences" heading. I chose not to do so in the book on ancient Greece because I needed a "gender roles" entry and because each would have retained gender-specific subentries in any case. I didn't think the text was sufficiently complex to warrant two gender-related entries, and the distinctions between them would probably have been lost on the book's intended audience. This relates to specificity as a guiding principle in finding a good balance in index writing. Many texts would indeed benefit from further differentiation. I chose not to use a "gender differences" heading in the book on the Lakota sweat lodge ceremony—but could have. The following is a simple example of combining "men" and "women" subentries under "gender differences," based on the Lakota anthropology quoted above:

gender differences
    in dressing for ceremony, 11
    in dress, 2-3
    location in lodge, 3
men. *See* gender; gender differences; women
women
    coming of age ceremony, 36, 287 n.18

contemporary accounts of, 65
ethnohistoric accounts of, 35, 40
interpretations and, variation in, 212
menstruation, 36, 202, 205 . . .
rebirth symbolism and, 205
segregation of, 80, 181, 205
sweats for, 207-209
See also gender; gender differences

Points of Analysis

Gender-related terms such as "gender differences" are analogous to the terms "ethnic differences" and "socioeconomic status"; all are gathering points for comparisons of complex social issues. As standard points of analysis so related, I sometimes cross-reference them to each other:

ethnic differences
See also . . . gender differences; socioeconomic status
gender differences
See also . . . ethnic differences; socioeconomic status
socioeconomic status
See also . . . ethnic differences; gender differences

Transsexuality

In Western culture, there is little provision for transsexuals, individuals whose genitals and identities as men or women are discordant (Strong and DeVault 1997, 27). The term "gender dysphoria" refers to this state. Currently in the transsexual culture, "transsexual" tends to refer to those who either are undergoing or wish to undergo hormonal and/or surgical intervention; "transgendered" is a term frequently used for those who experience the dissonance but are not necessarily taking the medical intervention route. Nevertheless, "transsexual" is used in both the transsexual culture and the psychological literature to indicate both experiences.

Many other cultures do make provision for this phenomenon, according the individuals high status and special privileges. "Two-spirit" has become a widely used term, both culturally and in the literature, to refer to such persons. "Berdache" has been derogatively used by Europeans and is not favored. Although the term "two-spirit" is Native American, it is cross-culturally understood. Other specific cultural words are the Indian *hija* and the Burmese *acault* (Strong and DeVault 1997, 27-28).

Transvestism should be not be confused with transsexuality. Also sometimes known as cross-dressing, transvestism is defined as the wearing of clothing by a member of the other sex for purposes of sexual arousal (Strong and DeVault 1997, 332). Technically, cross-dressing is different from transvestism (defined by a lack of sexual arousal), but specificity rarely justifies such a distinction; again, the text would define it if it were warranted.

Similarly, sexual orientation is a distinctly different phenomenon.

Sexual Orientation

Sensitivity to labels bids us use the term "sexual orientation" rather than "sexual preference"; although the terms are sometimes thought to be synonyms, the latter implies a choice that few people experience (APA 1994, 51). Building on the previous discussion of strategies for dealing with gender, "sexual orientation" is a useful gathering point for comparisons being made between heterosexuality and other orientations, as well as for information on the formation of, or social views on, orientation. I first try to gather subentries here rather than at "homosexuality" (for reasons I will detail later). I then place cross-references from bisexuality, heterosexuality, and homosexuality to sexual orientation. Depending on the complexity of the text, these main headings may or may not also carry subentries.

Bias: The Heterosexual Imperative

One difference in the normative assumptions and biases about sexual orientation compared to those about gender, of course, is that sexual orientation variations are numerical minorities, whereas with gender the numbers are equal. The development of these entries is, again, the result of their being regarded as out of the heterosexual norm of society, thus creating more discrete instances in the text. As with the male-as-norm discussion above, it is important to acknowledge point of view. If there is an entry for homosexuality, there should be an entry for heterosexuality, even if all that entry does is acknowledge the point of view of the text. I include a cross-reference from "heterosexuality" to homosexuality, "sexual orientation," or "sexuality," depending on the text.

An example of heterosexual bias in indexing was related to me by Margie Towery. She was asked to re-index a book; the first index had been rejected by the author because the indexer had been unequal in his treatment of issues. An instance of this is that on a page in which anal sex was discussed in terms of both heterosexuals and homosexuals, he had indexed only the references to homosexuals. While most indexers would like to assume ourselves to be above such bias, more subtle inequities are quite common in published indexes.

Bisexuality

Even if bisexuality is not specifically mentioned, a cross-reference from it to information on gay men or lesbians is a good use of the cross-reference tool as anticipation of the reader. Also, it is important to read the text carefully. The bi-phobia of both the heterosexual and homosexual universes is evidenced in the fact that many times what is discussed as homosexual behavior is actually bisexual behavior (*See also* the discussion of identity, below).

Gay Men and Lesbians vs. Homosexuality as a Term

If used strictly to represent same-gender sexual behavior and as a general descriptor of orientation (inclusive of social attitudes), the term "homosexuality" can be useful. However, the difficulties with the term are that it carries negative stereotypes, it carries few cultural referents, and it is ambiguous because it is understood by some to refer only to men. "Lesbians" and "gay men" are the specific and appropriate terms for identities, cultures, and communities. "Gay men" is preferable to "gay" because, again, gay is understood by some to refer only to men. Bisexuality and heterosexuality are used as both behavioral descriptors and identities (APA 1994, 51).

The following entries, from the text on the psychology of women previously quoted (Donelson 1998), illustrate how these concepts work together:

bisexuality, 386, 387-389, 394. *See also* sexual orientation
gay men. *See also* homosexuality; lesbians; sexual orientation
  ageing, 489
  and family,
    of choice, 508
    of origin, 367-368
    as parents, 173-174, 440
    siblings of, 390
  gender roles and, 363, 364
  hardships of, 366
  homophobia, 335, 338, 340, 366-367
  relationships of . . .
  [*and so on*]
heterosexuality. See also sexual orientation
  ageing, 405, 488
  children of lesbians and gays and, 173-174, 390-392
  choice and, 392, 394
  double standard of sexuality, 377
  marriage of partners. See marriage
  orgasm, 398, 403
  sexual liberation, 377-380, 385-386, 606
  [*and so on*]
homosexuality. See also bisexuality; gay men; lesbians; sexual orientation
  adolescence and, 377
  gender identity and, 363-365
  social organization and, 386
  theories of, 363, 389, 392-394
lesbians. See also gay men; homosexuality; sexual orientation
  ageing, 405, 488, 489
  AIDS, 381
  bisexuality and, 387-389
  breast cancer, 505
  as clergy, 620
  disability, 405, 406
  and family
    of choice, 368, 508
    of origin, 174, 367-368

        as parents, 173-174, 367, 390-392, 424
        siblings, 390
    feminism, 17, 395
    homophobia, 335, 338, 340 . . .
    identity of, 387-389, 392-394 . . .
    language stereotyping and, 67, 381
    legal system and, 174, 367, 518
    media depictions of, 52
    mental health care, 598
    minority women as, 367, 598
    [*and so on*]
sexual orientation. See also gay men; lesbians
    bisexuality, 386, 387-389, 394
    as changeable, 386-387, 389
    continuum of (Kinsey), 386-387
    gender identity and roles vs., 363
    heterosexuality. See heterosexuality
    homosexuality. See homosexuality
    mental health services and, 598
    parents' influence on, 173-174, 390-393
    same-sex genital exploration and, 374
    theories of, 363, 389, 392-394

In both the "homosexuality" and "sexual orientation" entries, the separation of homosexuality from gay men and lesbians in the cross-reference structures emphasizes that the latter are cultural groups, not defined solely by their sexual orientation. If the text is focused on cultural aspects and not on a technical discussion of sexuality, an entry for homosexuality may simply consist of a cross-reference to the cultural terms.

    homosexuality. *See* gay men; lesbians

For entries that always include both gay men and lesbians, an alternative is:

    gay men. See lesbians and gay men
    homosexuality. See lesbians and gay men
    lesbians and gay men
        [*subentries . . .*]

Or, one might choose to use the following word order: "gay men and lesbians."

Identity

Complicating the matter is the fact that the terms "lesbians" and "gay men" are relatively modern usages; *Webster's Collegiate Dictionary* (10th ed.) dates the terms at 1890 and 1953, respectively. A further complication is that a person may engage in same-gender sexual behaviors and still identify as heterosexual or may engage in male-female sexual behaviors and still identify as homosexual. Some historical figures have been called gay or lesbian by modern historians, whereas they may not have conceived of themselves as such. "Same-gender," "male-male," "female-female," and "male-female sexual behavior" (or sexual relations) are some terms that may be used to address these concerns (APA 1994, 51-52). In the previously quoted history of ancient Greece (Martin 1996), I addressed the historical problem by using the following entries:

> heterosexual relations, 66, 69, 79 . . .
> homosexual relations, 69, 78, 89 . . .
> sexual customs
>   and comedy, 164, 165
>   of the Cynics, 215
>   heterosexual, 66, 69, 79 . . .
>   homosexual, 69, 78, 89 . . .
>   See also love; marriage

This is an imperfect solution; although women are (briefly) discussed as having same-gender relations, women were not generally being referred to when the term was used in ancient Greece. The term "female homosexuality," however, was used in the book, which influenced my decision. Note that the term "sexual customs" was not used in the book. I chose it to encompass the group on sexuality, once again neutralizing a traditional bias, in this case, the heterosexual imperative.

Conclusions

Keeping in mind three organizational concepts—sensitivity to labels, specificity, and point of view—we may seek to provide entry points to our indexes that reflect the diversity of the index users. Indexers frequently must choose terms from among synonyms used by the author; careful choices based on these three organizational concepts can make the difference between an insular index and an accessible one. Finally, creative cross-referencing and main-heading formation add a new perspective on the material, part of the value we as indexers provide.

Acknowledgments

My thanks to Do Mi Stauber, Elsa Kramer, Margie Towery, and my spouse, Bill Rieben, for their comments on this text; any errors are my own.

Works Cited

American Psychological Association (APA). 1994. *Publication Manual of the American Psychological Association.* 4th ed. Washington, D.C.: APA.

Bucko, Raymond A. 1998. *The Lakota Ritual of the Sweat Lodge: History and Contemporary Practice.* Lincoln: University of Nebraska Press.

Donelson, Frances Elaine. 1998. *Women's Experiences: A Psychological Approach.* Mountain View, Calif.: Mayfield Publishing Company.

Judd, Karen. 1990. *Copyediting: A Practical Guide.* 2d ed. Los Altos, Calif.: Crisp Publications.

Martin, Thomas R. 1996. *Ancient Greece: From Prehistoric to Hellenistic Times.* New Haven, Conn.: Yale University Press.

Miller, Casey, and Kate Swift. 1988. *The Handbook of Nonsexist Writing: For Writers, Editors, and Speakers.* 2d ed. New York: Harper and Row.

Mulvany, Nancy C. 1994. *Indexing Books.* Chicago: University of Chicago Press.

Strong, Bryan, and Christine DeVault. 1997. *Human Sexuality.* 2d ed. Mountain View, Calif.: Mayfield Publishing Company.

HELPFUL REFERENCES ON HISTORY:
A GENERAL BIBLIOGRAPHY

American Psychological Association. 1994. *Publication Manual of the American Psychological Association.* 4th ed. Washington, D.C.: APA [helpful on language issues in general].

The Annals of America. 1968. Chicago: Encyclopaedia Brittanica.

Ballentine's Law Dictionary. 1969. 3d ed. Rochester, N.Y.: Lawyers Co-operative Publishing Company. Much of medieval history is law—land, its use and exchange, is the economic basis of feudal societies. *Ballentine's* covers terms both of common law-based and Roman law-based systems.

Baxter, J. H., and Charles Johnson. 1947. *A Medieval Latin Word-List.* London: Oxford University Press. An oldie but goody; probably still the most comprehensive and easy-to-use compilation of obscure medieval Latin terms and variant spellings.

Bethell, Leslie, ed. 1984-95. *Cambridge History of Latin America.* 11 vols. New York: Cambridge University Press. Though the indexes in each volume contain occasional flaws, the series of eleven paperbacks is an excellent in-depth reference work.

Blackburn, Simon. 1996. *The Oxford Dictionary of Philosophy.* New York: Oxford University Press. Good, concise summaries of both ancient and modern schools of thought; useful for looking up both medieval philosophies mentioned in a text and for understanding the scholarly theory upon which the author's ideas are based.

Blackwell Dictionary of Judaica. 1992. Oxford: Blackwell Publishing. Jewish history remains an important subject for medieval and Renaissance scholars; *Blackwell's* is particularly good at describing how Jewish customs have changed through time.

Bothamley, Jennifer. 1993. *Dictionary of Theories.* Detroit, Mich.: Gale Research. Like the *Oxford Dictionary of Philosophy,* this reference work covers a multitude of thought systems; probably better for modern theory and for more loosely organized schools of thought that don't quite rate as philosophies.

The Cambridge Encyclopedia of Latin America and the Caribbean. 1992. 2d ed. New York: Cambridge University Press.

The Cambridge Factfinder. 1993. New York: Cambridge University Press.

The Chicago Manual of Style. 1993. 14th ed. Chicago: University of Chicago Press. Helpful in deciding how to index foreign names and things like musical compositions, art works, and so on.

Chilvers, Ian, ed. 1997. *The Concise Oxford Dictionary of Art and Artists.* Oxford: Oxford University Press.

Chilvers, Ian, Harold Osborne, and Dennis Farr, eds. 1994. *The Oxford Dictionary of Art.* Oxford: Oxford University Press. A dictionary of international museums and galleries with more than 3,000 entries on Western painting, sculpture, drawing, graphic arts, and applied arts, treating artists, schools, periods, techniques, critical terms, and so on.

The Concise Columbia Encyclopedia. 1994. 3d ed. New York: Columbia University Press. Great for checking details of political events and actors.

Diamond, David, ed. 1992. *The Bulfinch Pocket Dictionary of Art Terms.* Boston: Little, Brown. Includes concise definitions for over 900 items, drawings describing architectural elements, and a bibliography.

Dictionary of National Biography. 1917–present. London: Oxford University Press. Usually known as the DNB and updated on a regular basis since its inception, this publication contains substantial biographies of all well-known and many obscure historical figures. Your library will probably have a mixture of editions in its set; even the oldest volumes are pretty reliable.

Drabble, Margaret, ed. 1985. *The Oxford Companion to English Literature.* 5th ed. London: Oxford University Press. Full of useful tidbits and fascinating information, a must for the indexer working in literature-based history. Despite the title, it contains lots of material on non-English European literature.

Dumond, Val. 1990. *A Guide to Inclusive Spoken and Written English.* New York: Prentice-Hall.

Encyclopaedia Britannica. 1979, 1990. Chicago: Encyclopaedia Britannica.

Farmer, David Hugh. 1997. *The Oxford Dictionary of Saints.* New York: Oxford University Press. Need details about a saint's life? Trying to distinguish one St. Catherine from another? Confused (and revolted) by methods of torturing virgin martyrs or puzzled by the meaning of symbols used to represent certain saints? This is the place to look.

Guidelines for Bias-Free Usage. 1993. N.p.: Association of American University Presses. A useful guide, but keep in mind that preferred terminology changes and indexers need to keep up with appropriate language use in the areas they work in.

The HarperCollins Dictionary of Biography. 1993. New York: HarperCollins.

Jerusalem Bible. 1966. London: Darton Longman and Todd. You can't understand the Middle Ages, Renaissance, or any European history without some grasp of the Bible. I like the *Jerusalem* because it's a clear translation with extremely good notes (If you're tempted to use your King James version, remember, it's a seventeenth-century translation—not medieval or Renaissance.).

Judd, Karen. 1990. *Copyediting: A Practical Guide.* 2d ed. Los Altos, Calif.: Crisp Publications.

Kelly, J. N. D. 1988. *The Oxford Dictionary of Popes.* New York: Oxford University Press. Popes are almost but not quite as confusing as saints. This book is particularly useful for sorting out the different names used for the same priest as he passes from plain old Father Joe Smith to Monsignor to Bishop to Archbishop to Pope.

Lewis, Charlton T., and Charles Short. 1975. *A Latin Dictionary.* Oxford: Clarendon Press. Still the best Latin dictionary around.

Mayer, Ralph. 1995. *Dictionary of Art Terms and Techniques.* New York: HarperCollins. Covers all forms of easel and mural painting, drawing, sculpture, graphic arts, photography, ceramics, and mosaics; contains over 3,200 well-defined terms encountered in the study and practice of visual arts.

Merriam-Webster's Collegiate Dictionary. 1993. 10th ed. Springfield, Mass.: Merriam-Webster. Good source for American spellings and terminology commonly used by American authors.

Merriam-Webster's Geographical Dictionary. 1997. 3d ed. Springfield, Mass.: Merriam-Webster. This is the latest edition and contains, for example, the newly formed countries in eastern Europe.

Miller, Casey, and Kate Swift. 1988. *The Handbook of Nonsexist Writing: For Writers, Editors, and Speakers.* 2d ed. New York: Harper and Row.

Morehead, Philip D., with Anne MacNeil. 1991. *The New American Dictionary of American Music.* New York: Dutton. Another source for names, including musicians' nicknames, as well as names of some musical compositions.

The Mosby Medical Encyclopedia. 1992. New York: Penguin.

Mulvany, Nancy. 1994. *Indexing Books.* Chicago: University of Chicago Press.

Murray, Peter, and Linda Murray. 1992. *Penguin Dictionary of Art and Artists.* New York: Penguin. Simply a classic.

The New York Public Library Book of Popular Americana. 1994. New York: Macmillan.

The New York Public Library Desk Reference. 1993. New York: Prentice-Hall.

Oxford Dictionary of the Christian Church. 1997. 3d ed. Oxford: Oxford University Press. Probably the best source available for information about theology, ecclesiology, hagiography, heresy, and church history.

Oxford English Dictionary. I use two for tracking down British spelling and terminology and for archaic English usage: *The Concise Oxford Dictionary.* 1990. Oxford: Clarendon Press, a one-volume, 50,000 word dictionary comparable to *Webster's Collegiate,* and *The Compact Edition of the Oxford English Dictionary.* 1971. Oxford: Oxford University Press, the entire multivolume OED squeezed into two fine-print, oversized volumes (it comes with a magnifying glass). The OED was re-edited in 1990, and a CD-ROM version is available (around $900), but the

Compact is readily available in second-hand stores for a surprisingly reasonable cost, allowing you to have it at home. The *Compact* OED is particularly useful for obscure and archaic words and for etymologies of words; the *Concise* OED is good for modern terms.

Previté-Orton, C. W. 1971. *Shorter Cambridge Medieval History.* 2 vols. Cambridge: Cambridge University Press. Available in most public libraries and in paperback at your local bookstore, these are extremely handy reference volumes, beautifully written, and easy to use.

Smith, James. 1998. *From Abacus to Zeus: A Handbook of Art History.* Englewood Cliffs, N.J.: Prentice-Hall.

Storey, R. L. 1973. *Chronology of the Medieval World, 800-1491.* New York: David Mackay. Forget whether Bosworth Field was before or after the death of Edward IV? This is the place to look.

Strayer, Joseph R., ed. 1985. *Dictionary of the Middle Ages.* New York: Charles Scribner's Sons. A good quick reference for confusing terms, dates, and historical summations.

Strunk, William, Jr., and E. B. White. 1979. *The Elements of Style.* 3d ed. New York: Macmillan. Always a good reminder on using precise language; my edition advertises on its cover, "With Index."

Tenenbaum, Barbara A., ed. 1996. *Encyclopedia of Latin American History and Culture.* New York: Charles Scribner's Sons.

Valk, Barbara, ed. 1989. *HAPI Thesaurus and Name Authority, 1970-1989.* Los Angeles: University of California, Latin American Center.

Webster's New Biographical Dictionary. 1988. Springfield, Mass.: Merriam-Webster. A big help in figuring out all those names.

Webster's New World Encyclopedia, Pocket Edition. 1993. New York: Prentice-Hall.

CONTRIBUTORS

Victoria Baker studied with Nancy Mulvany at UC Berkeley Extension in 1989 before a stint being mentored as a law indexer. She holds a B.A. in art and a certificate in technical writing. A generalist, she now indexes textbooks and scholarly works in several fields, including anthropology (multidisciplinary works a specialty), philosophy, psychology, history, and alternative medicine. For relaxation, she occasionally enjoys indexing math and science. Victoria lives with her spouse and several rescued animal companions, enjoys horticulture and making music, and counsels people who are dealing with death and dying. After nearly twenty years in San Francisco, she finally took her freelance indexing to where she always meant for it to take her: northern California.

Diane Brenner has a degree in art history from Brandeis University. Though she has abandoned the arts for a professional career in the sciences, she has maintained her interest in fine arts and crafts through reading and the practice of embroidery, weaving, beadwork, and rug hooking. Nine years ago she began a new career as an indexer. A generalist, she has been fortunate to have the opportunity to index several art history books. She lives in Worthington, Massachusetts.

Francine Cronshaw has graduate degrees in Latin American history and has pursued post-doctoral studies in education. Besides teaching history at the college level, she has done extensive research on agriculture and political economy topics. Her publications in academic and journalistic venues have appeared in English and Spanish. Francine's day job is as a full-time indexer, translator, and editor.

Kate Mertes earned her B.A. in medieval studies from Mount Holyoke College and a Ph.D. in medieval English history from the University of Edinburgh (Scotland). After teaching at the university level, she moved into publishing. Kate has been indexing for over twenty years, starting with a fellow undergraduate's thesis. After stints with Oxford University Press and Andromeda Press in Britain, Kate returned to the United States in 1990. She currently runs the indexing department for RIAG's human resources division in Alexandria, Virginia, freelance indexes; and writes screenplays on the side.

Marilyn Rowland indexes a wide variety of books and particularly enjoys indexing art and art history books. She has learned about art by taking classes in drawing and painting, by reading widely, by indulging in arts and crafts of all kinds, and by teaching classes in art appreciation as a parent volunteer to elementary school students. She has twenty-five years of experience as an indexer and lives in Falmouth, Massachusetts.

Sandy Topping learned indexing as an indexer's assistant in 1985. In 1989, she went to work at Carnegie-Mellon University and indexed part-time. In 1992, she decided that it was time to try her act without a net, and she left CMU for full-time indexing. She indexes primarily textbooks and is a generalist, preferring a variety of topics—history, medicine, social sciences, law, and so on. Her husband, Glenn, fends for himself quite well when she's working. Her sons, Michael and Andrew, were almost grown when she began indexing—they aided her efforts by leaving home so she could have some office space. Her furry assistants, Bunny, Morganna, Indiana, and Harley, are in charge of notifying her when it's dinnertime. Her favorite historical event is the defenestration of Prague. She personally doubts that angels had anything to do with the outcome—and strongly favors the manure-pile theory.

Margie Towery has a graduate degree in history, attained after her two daughters had started school. In addition to experience in archival work and historical research, she has worked in publishing for over a decade and has been indexing for five years, after finally discovering that indexing was what she wanted to do "when she grew up." She works primarily for scholarly presses and, while she considers herself a generalist, most enjoys indexing books in social sciences, women's studies, history, sociology, and literary criticism. Her writing, including poetry and nonfiction, has been published in anthologies and academic venues. Margie's nonindexing life includes a passion (though little time) for quilting. She had a one-woman show of her quilts in 1997.

INDEX

by Margie Towery

Abbott, Berenice, 33
Accent marks, 12–13
Africa, periodization in, 2–3
Alliance for Progress, 11
Alphabetization
  art and art history, 32–33
  Latin American history, 12–14
  medieval and Renaissance history, 6–7
Appliqué needlework, thesaurus entry for, 35–36
Architectural history
  combined with biography, 34
  thesaurus as resource on, 35–36
  titles of structures in, 31
Area studies, focus of, 11
Art and art history
  audience for, 34
  background needed for, 27
  illustrations in, 29–31
  learning about, 28, 34
  Middle Ages and Renaissance, 3
  names in, 29–34
  print references for, 32–33, 35–38
  publishers of, 27–29
  terminology and concepts in, 27–29, 34–36
  thesauri as resources on, 35–36
  titles of works in, 29–31
  Web references for, 33, 35, 38–39
Asia, periodization in, 2–3
Audience
  art and art history, 34
  language considerations and, 48, 53
  medieval and Renaissance history, 3
  textbooks, 17
Austria, name of, 21–22

Battles, 20
Biographies, 3, 7–8, 34
Bisexuality, use of term, 50–51
Books. *See also* Art and art history; Latin
  American history; Medieval and Renaissance
  history; Publishers; Textbooks

essay collections, 4, 8, 35
monographs, 4, 15
titles of, 13
Brueghel (Bruegel), Pieter, the Elder, 32
Buckingham, Duke of, 7

Capitalization, 13
Cassatt, Mary, 31
Chicago Manual of Style, 29
Chipman, Alison, 35–36
Christine de Pizan, 5, 6
Cities, names of, 21
Civil War (U.S.), 19–20
Cold war, influence of, 11
Countries, names of, 22
Cross-references
  concepts/events, 19–20
  countries, 22
  gender considerations in, 41, 43–49
  location of, v
  names, 6–7, 33
  neighborhood analogy, vi
  sexual orientation considerations in, 50–53
  subentries, from, 20, 52
  terminology, 5–6, 8, 34–36

Dark Ages, 1
Dates. *See also* Periodization
  artworks, 30
  battle entries, 20
  countries, 21–22
  name entries, 19
Degas, Edgar, 30
Disease, in medieval and Renaissance history,
  3–4

Early modern period, 2
El Greco (Domenicos Theotocopoulos), 32–33
England
  law in, 5

61

periodization in, 1–2
Essay collections
    length of, 4
    terminology in, 8, 35
Ethnic differences, use of term, 49
Europe
    periodization in, 1–3
    place-names in, 21
Exhibition, use of term, 31
Explanatory notes, 32, 34

Family history, 4
Female, definition of, 42
Female homosexuality, use of term, 53
Frederick William, identification of, 18–19

García Márquez, Gabriel, 13
Gay men, use of term, 41, 50–52
Gender. *See also* women
    definition of, 42–43
    men as norm in, 43–44, 46
    terminology for, 41–49
    women as point of view, 44–46
Gender differences, use of term, 43–44, 48–49
Gender dysphoria, explanation of, 49
Gender roles, definition of, 43
Getty Information Institute, 33, 35
Gogh, Vincent Van, 33
Gombrich, E. H., The Story of Art, 32
Gostelow, Mary, Embroidery, 32
Greece, gender in, 46–47, 53

Hartt, Frederick, Art History of Painting,
    Sculpture, and Architecture, 34
Headnotes, 32, 34
Henry I (King of England), 7
Henry I (King of France), 7
Henry IV (King of England), 8
Heterosexuality, use of term, 50–53
High Middle Ages, 2, 6
Hockney, David, 31
Homosexuality, use of term, 41, 50–53

Ideology, research interests affected by, 12
Illustrations, 29–31
Indexes. *See also* Alphabetization; Cross-
    references; Page locators; Subentries
    complex vs. simple entries in, 19–20

editing, 21–23, 25–26
    headnotes for, 32, 34
    lack of, 27
    neighborhood analogy for, vi
    previous editions of, 17
    scattered mentions in, 20
    stylistic considerations in, v, 4, 11, 13, 15,
        26–27, 29

Journals, as resources, 4

Kennedy, John F., 11

Lakota Sioux, gender in, 47–49
Language. *See also* Terminology
    medieval and Renaissance history, 4–5
    Portuguese, 11–14
    Spanish, 11–14
    terms borrowed from another, 36
Late Antique period, 1
Latin American history
    academic field, 11–12
    content of, 14–15
    names in, 12–14
    references on, 12–15
Lawrence, Jacob, 30
Lesbians, use of term, 41, 50–52

Male, definition of, 42
Margaret of Anjou, 6
Márquez, Gabriel García. *See* García Márquez,
    Gabriel
Medieval and Renaissance history
    audience for, 3
    language issues in, 4–5
    learning about, 3–4, 9
    names in, 6–8
    periodization in, 1–3
    references on, 9
    spelling in, 5–7
    terminology in, 4–8
Men. *See also* Gay men; Gender
    definition of, 42
    norm, as, 43–44, 46
Michelangelo Buonarroti, 31, 33
Middle East, periodization in, 2–3
Miller, Casey, 43
Monet, Claude, 30–31

Monographs
    Latin American history, 15
    length of, 4

Names. *See also* Place-names; Titles
    art and art history, 29–34
    cross-references for, 6–7, 33
    Latin American history, 12–14
    medieval and Renaissance history, 6–8
    separate index for, 25
    textbooks, in, 18–20
Normalization of violence, 8
North America, periodization in, 2–3

Page locators
    number of, 20*n*4, 22
    special typography for, 29–31, 34
Page proofs
    arrival of, 25
    corrections/typos/inconsistencies in, 12–13,
        25, 33
    marking, 18, 25
    received in batches, 17
Periodization, 1–3
Picasso, Pablo, 29–30
Pizan, Christine de. *See* Christine de Pizan
Place-names
    Spanish, 12
    textbooks, in, 21–22
Portuguese language, 11–14
Publishers
    art and art history, 27–29
    content guidelines from, 15
    foreign language issues and, 12–13
    space limits set by, 23, 30
    style guidelines from, v, 4, 11, 13, 15, 26–27,
        29

"Quiting," 5–6

Raleigh (Ralegh), Sir Walter, 5
Reformation, 2
Rembrandt, 32
Renaissance history. *See* Medieval and
    Renaissance history
Robert the Gross, 6
Rossi, Properzia de', 33
Russia, periodization in, 2

Saints, 7
Scandinavia, periodization in, 2
Scheduling, considerations in, 25
Seneca society, 44
Series, use of term, 31
Sex/sex roles, definition of, 42–43
Sexual customs, use of term, 53
Sexual dimorphism, definition of, 42
Sexual orientation
    bias and, 50
    identity and, 52–53
    terminology for, 41–42, 50–53
Socioeconomic status, use of term, 49
South America, periodization in, 2–3
Spanish language, 11–14
Specialization, argument for, 14
Spelling, in medieval and Renaissance history,
    5–7. *See also* Names
States, names of, 21
Subentries
    Cross-references from, 20, 52
    Editing process, 22–23
    Identifying type of, 18, 21
    Order of, 31
Swift, Kate, 43

Teal, John, 6
Terminology
    art and art history, 27–29, 34–36
    cross-references for, 5–6, 8, 34–36
    flexibility in, 41
    "foreign," 13, 32
    gender considerations in, 41–49
    idiosyncratic, 5–6, 8
    italicized, 13, 32
    medieval and Renaissance history, 4–6, 8
    sexual orientation considerations in, 41–42,
        50–53
    thesauri as resources for, 35–36
Textbooks
    audience for, 17
    editing indexes for, 21–23
    Latin American history, 15
    names in, 18–20
    place-names in, 21–22
    process for indexing, 17, 25–26
    project worksheet for, 17–18, 24
    references on, 18, 21, 26

splits for versions of, 23
structure of, 18, 23
Thesauri, 35–36
Thomas Aquinas, 6–7
Titles
  art works, 29–31
  books and articles, 13
  buildings, 31
  people, 7
Title VI, creation and effect of, 11–12
Transsexuality, explanation of, 49
Transvestism, explanation of, 49
"Two-spirit," explanation of, 49

United States, place-names in, 21
University of California, Los Angeles, Latin

American Center at, 14
Untitled, use of term, 31

Valk, Barbara, 14
Van Dyke (Vandyke), Sir Anthony, 32
Van Gogh, Vincent. *See* Gogh, Vincent Van

Wayne, John, 6
  Web, art and art history references on, 33, 35,
    38–39
Women. *See also* Gender; Lesbians
  definition of, 42
  history of, 3, 8, 46
  index for psychology text on, 45–46, 51–52
  point of view of, 44–46
Wright, Frank Lloyd, 35

Other Books on Indexing from ASI and Information Today, Inc.

Can You Recommend a Good Book on Indexing?

By Bella Hass Weinberg ($39.50/150 pp/ISBN 1-57387-041-2)

Cataloging Heresy

Edited by Bella Hass Weinberg ($35.00/270 pp/ISBN 0-938734-60-1)

Challenges in Indexing Electronic Text and Images

Edited by Fidel, Hahn, Rasmussen, and Smith ($39.50/316 pp/ISBN 0-938734-76-8)

Directory of Indexing and Abstracting Courses and Seminars

Edited by Maryann Corbett

($12.00 reg.,$18.00 ASI members/40 pp/ISBN 1-57387-056-0)

A Glossary

By Hans H. Wellisch ($16.00 reg.,$10.00 ASI members/64 pp/ISBN 0-936547-35-9)

An Indexer's Guide to the Internet

By Lori Lathrop ($15.00 reg.,$10.00 ASI members/40 pp/ISBN 0-936547-22-7)

Indexing: The State of Our Knowledge and the State of Our Ignorance

Edited by Bella Hass Weinberg ($30.00/134 pp/ISBN 0-938734-32-6)

Marketing Your Indexing Services—Second Edition

Edited by Anne Leach

($20.00 reg.,$15.00 ASI members/70 pp/ISBN 1-57387-054-4)

Running Your Indexing Business

($15.00 reg.,$20.00 ASI members/42 pp/ISBN 0-936547-32-4)

Starting an Indexing Business—Second Edition

($25.00 reg.,$30.00 ASI members/106 pp/ISBN 0-936547-31-6)

To order directly from the publisher, include $3.95 postage and handling for the first book ordered
and $3.25 for each additional book. Catalogs also available upon request.

Information Today, Inc., 143 Old Marlton Pike,
Medford, NJ 08055 • (609)654-6266